TRUE PROSPERITY

TRUE PROSPERITY

JAMES ROBISON

TYNDALE HOUSE PUBLISHERS, INC.
WHEATON, ILLINOIS

Visit Tyndale's exciting Web site at www.tyndale.com

True Prosperity

Copyright © 2004 by James Robison. All rights reserved.

Designed by Luke Daab

Edited by Dave Lindstedt

Library of Congress Cataloging-in-Publication Data

Robison, James, date.
    True prosperity / James Robison.
        p. cm.
    Includes bibliographical references.
    ISBN 1-4143-0029-8 (hc)
    1. Wealth—Religious aspects—Christianity. 2. Christian giving. I. Title.
    BR115.W4R64 2004
    241'.68—dc22   2004011385

Printed in the United States of America

10 09 08 07 06 05
7   6   5   4

TABLE OF CONTENTS

BLESSED IN LIFE

*Discernment is not a matter of simply telling the
difference between right and wrong; rather, it is telling
the difference between right and almost right.*

CHARLES H. SPURGEON

My WIFE, Betty, and I are truly blessed in life. We
recently celebrated our fortieth anniversary, and it
is beautiful to watch our three children love their
spouses, communicate openly, parent their children
wisely, and prosper in their lives. This is not to suggest
that they don't face challenges, but the beauty we
observe in their responses to the ups and downs of life
thrills us beyond measure. Just as Betty and I have
learned to do, our children face their challenges with
confidence, and they tackle life's lessons with abiding
peace in their hearts. No amount of money or worldly
success can provide what we witness in our own lives
and in those of our children.

I believe that our loving heavenly Father wants to

bless us in this lifetime. I believe it because I read it in his Word, and I know it is true because I have experienced it in my own life and have observed it clearly in the lives of many others. Nevertheless, we must be clear about what we mean by "God's blessing" because in our society, and within the church, many people are caught up in a mad pursuit of an improperly defined prosperity that leaves most people empty and unfulfilled. Never have *so many* chased *so much* and come up with *so little* of real value. It breaks my heart. It reminds me of some rosebushes I have seen that bloom large, beautiful flowers, then come crashing down to the ground because their roots are not deep enough to support the weight.

Over the years, I have earnestly sought answers from God and in his Word in order to share some realistic answers to key questions about true prosperity:

- Amid the circumstances of life, why are Betty and I so blessed and full of peace?
- How did I, a boy born as the product of a forced sexual relationship and raised in poverty, find such success, personal joy, and even monetary blessing?
- Can everyone enjoy the same spiritual, emotional, and material prosperity that I have?

◆ Can I share God's truth in ways that will help others find true
  prosperity?

Even though I grew up in a dysfunctional home with
unstable parents and living conditions bordering on
abject poverty, I never felt shortchanged in life. Even
before I became a Christian, I never believed that God
had overlooked me.

Certainly, I noticed people who were wealthy or successful by the world's standard of measure, but I never
coveted what they had, and I never begrudged them
their material success. I never felt that the world owed
me something. I never felt that God had mistreated me.
I was grateful for what little I did have. I can honestly
say, as the apostle Paul says in Philippians 4:11-12, that
I was content in every circumstance.

I believe that this foundation of contentment with
what God has provided in my life is one of the reasons
that I still have an overwhelming sense of gratitude
now that I have experienced some monetary blessings
in life. At the same time, if every material blessing was
taken away from me, I would still enjoy true prosperity,
the real essence of life, which comes from my relationship with almighty God.

In my travels throughout the United States and
around the world, I've noticed that those who harbor

resentment or feelings of being shortchanged in life and those who bear a spirit of covetousness actually block God's blessing in their lives by their attitudes. Because they believe that God, or life in general, has not treated them fairly, they seldom honor God with the things they do have in their lives. Instead of accepting God's grace with a grateful heart, they cut off his blessings with their negative mind-set.

If you have bought into the idea that God—or life— owes you something and you're getting the short end of the stick, then you have constructed a major roadblock in your path to prosperity. Covetousness and resentment block your ability to see clearly and discern wisely. These issues must be rooted out and dealt with.

It is my deep conviction that deliverance from these unhealthy attitudes and thoughts clears a person's mind to exercise sound judgment and make wise decisions, including those related to investments and financial opportunity.

Over the past forty years I have spoken with many people who have achieved true prosperity in life. I want to share with you what I learned from them. Also, the Lord has shown me many things in life—choices made, attitudes maintained, temptations resisted, relationships developed—that lead to true prosperity. I have put these key elements in writing to help you realize the blessings the Lord has in store for you.

Sometimes just a few, simple ideas can completely change your life. For example, learning how to be a river instead of a reservoir. Or learning how to *scale down* in order to *step up*. Or perhaps you need to learn how to identify and remove major obstacles to prosperity.

The truths that I share in this book come with the confidence that God's will is to bless you beyond anything you could ever imagine—not just monetarily but in ways that are priceless.

Throughout my life, whenever I have experienced something exciting or meaningful, I have wanted to share it with others. I have never been one to hoard, whether it's ideas or material resources. I've always thought, *Let's enjoy it together. Let's share it.* This was true even when I was a child and lived in poverty. I wanted to share what little I had. I believe that God took note of my heart's attitude. (And believe me, he knows how and when to repay.) This inner attitude is just one critically important way to tap into a spiritual power source that can shape our lives.

I do not seek prosperity. I seek God's will in my life, and prosperity finds me. True prosperity.

CHAPTER 1

WHAT IS TRUE PROSPERITY?

WE MUST move beyond thinking of prosperity in purely monetary or materialistic terms. Limiting our concept of abundance to finances ignores the wealth of time, gifts, and abilities that mark truly successful people. True prosperity is having all the resources we need to fulfill God's purpose for our lives and the abiding peace and joy that enable us to be perfectly content in abundance or while facing grave challenges. True prosperity is "joy inexpressible and full of glory" (1 Peter 1:8, NASB). It is possible only when we are absolutely convinced that

> When the prosperity message is put in its proper place, it allows us to become everything that God wants us to be.

God—in whom we trust explicitly and exclusively—will "meet all your needs according to his glorious riches" (Philippians 4:19). We must be delivered from defining our desires as needs. God alone truly understands needs, and he is most anxious to meet them.

Once we discover what prosperity really is, we can find personal fulfillment and spiritual effectiveness regardless of our circumstances. When the prosperity message is put in its proper place, it allows us to become everything that God wants us to be. He wants us to be prosperous in this life—even as our souls prosper—but we must come to clearly understand prosperity from God's viewpoint. It's not about getting rich; it's about living richly. It's not about gaining wealth; it's about learning the true meaning of wealth and prosperity.

Dr. Tony Evans has been a guest on our television program, *Life Today*, numerous times. Recently, as we were discussing his book *God Is More Than Enough*, I said to the television audience, "You're really going to get blessed when you bless others. Isn't that right, Tony?"

"Absolutely," Dr. Evans replied. "You can't outgive God."

"That doesn't mean he's going to give you a money tree, though," I said. "He's going to give you what money can't buy."

Then Dr. Evans uttered a short but profound statement that captures the essence of true prosperity: "He's going to give you himself."

That is the wealth that God promises: riches in Christ.

THE PURSUIT OF HAPPINESS

Everyone wants to be happy, but not many people seem to experience what their hearts long for. Happiness, however, is not beyond our reach. We can live meaningful lives filled with peace and joy, even though we still have mountains to climb and obstacles to overcome. Through it all, it is possible to live an abundant, joy-filled life.

Let me state it in the most emphatic way possible: *God desires to bless everyone.*

He longs for us to experience the fullness of his love, grace, and true prosperity. He loves to lavishly reward faithful followers and stewards. He pours out blessings on his family, those who trust him, the children he loves, and even some who resist his divine guidance, wisdom, and care. He wants us to continually experience his boundless, limitless love. God's own Son, Jesus, said that he came to give us *abundance of life.* Tragically, this great promise and eternal truth is misunderstood by the majority of people throughout the world to mean abundance *in* life. It is undeniable and easy to observe that material prosperity and monetary gain do not bring real meaning in life. Simply being wealthy is not true prosperity.

Material prosperity and monetary gain do not bring real meaning in life. Simply being wealthy is not true prosperity. In a recently published book, *The Progress Paradox: How Life Gets Better While People Feel Worse,* Gregg Easterbrook answers the question of whether materialism brings happiness. "The answer, unequivocally, is no," he says. In fact, even though middle-class men and women in the United States and the European Union have a higher standard of living than 99.4 percent of people who have ever lived, Easterbrook says, by and large they "walk around scowling rather than smiling at their good fortune."[1] The all-too-common sight of people driving their luxury automobiles into gated subdivisions to unload their recent purchases, yet living with frowns on their faces, reveals the vanity and futility of the endless pursuit of wealth and materialism.

David Myers, a sociologist at Hope College in Michigan, shared research that indicated more Americans were happier in the 1940s, when one-third of the population still used outhouses. The reason, he says, is obvious: "By the end of the 1990s, we were excelling at making a living but too often failing to make a life."[2]

Author and philosopher Henry David Thoreau once observed that far too many people come to the end of their lives and discover they really have not lived at all. The problem, says anticonsumerism activist Kalle Lasn, is that we have been conditioned to believe that yesterday's luxuries are today's necessities. North Americans are bombarded by three thousand marketing messages a day. Essentially, they all communicate the same message: "You can be happy by buying something."[3] In other words, the key to life is getting. This flies in the face of the wisdom imparted by the greatest teacher who ever walked the planet. He said, "It is more blessed to give than to receive" (Acts 20:35, NASB). Still, most people in the developed world continue their mad pursuit of material gain thinking it will provide a better life.

When I was still in my twenties, I conducted a crusade in the oil-boom cities of Midland and Odessa in west Texas. One night after the meeting I was eating dinner with a ministry associate, soloist John McKay, in a local restaurant. Seated a short distance from us were six couples, who were having a very open and loud conversation. One man commented, "I've lost over $5 million in the last two weeks!" Another claimed that he'd had a similar setback. Both went on to say, however, that their financial strength was apparently unshakable, even through their recent loss and frustration. As the evening wore on, it became obvious that their brave words masked a sense of longing and emptiness. Despite their monetary success, a void existed deep down in their souls.

After listening to this materialistic exchange, I stood up, walked over to the far end of the table, and addressed the group with a confident, yet compassionate, firmness. "Excuse me, please," I said. "I couldn't help but overhear your conversation about your material well-being. I thought that because you were discussing such large sums of money, I would take this opportunity to introduce you to the wealthiest young man in the world.

"Yes, that's right," I continued quite forcefully. "I am the wealthiest young man in the world. *But I don't have a lot of money.* I have that which money can never provide. I grew up in total, abject poverty, without a father, and yet at this moment I am filled with joy and peace beyond my ability to adequately describe. All the success the world offers can never provide this, but I have found it—and there's nothing in this world that can take it away."

I turned abruptly, walked past the table, past my associate, out the door, and stepped into the courtesy car provided by the churches that were sponsoring the crusade. After my departure, John McKay sat quietly and listened to the couples' response. One of the women exclaimed, "God, he's got guts!" Another woman spoke up, "Yes, but I believe he was sincere. He seemed so real. I think he meant it." One of the men who had discussed his losses said, "I do, too. Somehow I believe he cared." He turned to my associate and asked, "Who was that?"

John answered, "Well, he's just who he said he was. He's a young man who lives in abundance of life." Ultimately John went on to explain that I was a guest minister speaking in a community-wide outreach and that I had found life through a total commitment to Jesus Christ. I believe in that brief moment this group heard profound truth about what is genuinely important in life.

The Fort Worth *Star-Telegram* reported in a March 17, 2004, article titled "The Burden of Materialism" that many social scientists now say that "research is more and more conclusive that people with many close friends and those in committed relationships are much more likely to be happy."[4] Researchers also found that "membership in a faith community greatly improves our chances" of happiness in life.[5] The sooner we learn the following truth, the happier we will be: *If you want to experience life fully, begin to express life freely.*

However insignificant you consider your resources to be, you have been entrusted with time, talent, and material possessions that you can share with others who have specific needs. You have been blessed so that you can have a positive impact on the lives of people around you and those who are suffering throughout the world.

If you want to experience life fully, begin to express life freely.

Betty and I have experienced what the world calls success—even monetarily. The amazing thing is that possessions have never brought us the joy we experience daily, nor have they been allowed to rob us of joy. The real issue today is not whether we can live without monetary abundance but whether we can live *with* it. God has promised to meet our needs, but we must understand that he is the one who accurately *defines* our needs. Our *desires*, however strong they may be, do not necessarily correspond to our *needs*.

In ancient Israel, after years of being governed by a series of judges, the people wanted a king. They thought they needed one. After all, every other nation had one. The fact is, it was the last thing they really needed. But God gave them a king. It proved to be one of the worst things that ever happened. May God deliver us from misinterpreting our desires as legitimate needs. As I said before, Jesus promised an abundant life, not necessarily abundance *in* life. I have found that God, in love, often withholds abundance of things because he knows we cannot handle the abundance. He knows that often material gain will distract us from what is eternal and meaningful and we will end up putting our wealth ahead of our love for God.

On the other hand, if you have been led to believe that by putting God first—even becoming a Christian who shares—you will somehow obligate God to pour out monetary blessings on you even though your spiritual life is undernourished and you lack maturity, then you have also bought into a deception. If while reading this book you find my suggestion to reexamine your belief system offensive, then you above all need to take a hard look at your theology.

The apostle Paul said, "Flee idols" (1 Corinthians 10:14, my paraphrase). Why? Because if we have idols, they will tend to have us. The problem that many people face when they experience monetary success is not that they own possessions but that the possessions *own them*. Remember the rich ruler who asked Christ what to do to inherit eternal life? (see Mark 10:17-31; Luke 18:18-30). When Jesus told him to sell what he owned and give to the poor, the man "went sadly away because he had many possessions" (Mark 10:22, NLT).

The truth is, *his many possessions had him*. Paul warns us that when we tolerate idols, we have "fellowship with demons" (1 Corinthians 10:20, NKJV). We can even hold on to a theological truth with an attitude that makes an idol out of the teaching or the teacher, and we will find that it produces a very unholy spirit in us. The Holy Spirit always produces the fruit of life. God's Spirit is always redemptive, whereas the spirit of darkness is always destructive. This includes judgmentalism, legalism, criticism, and exalting humanity's ideas above God's liberating truth.

There is often greater peace and contentment among the people of impoverished, developing nations than there is in the prosperous communities of the United States.

Never have so many pursued so much and come up with so little. Look around and you will see that this is true. I have seen it time and again all around the world. In my travels, it has been interesting for me to note that there is often greater peace and contentment among the people of impoverished, developing nations than there is in the prosperous communities of the United States. As a matter of fact, I can show you more misery per square foot in a suburban country club setting than you will see in many inner-city ghettos. In our feeding centers throughout Africa,* children who have regained enough strength to play have more fun playing with a rock than many American children have at entertainment parks, playgrounds, or through all the opportunities afforded them through community sports leagues. You'll see more smiles on the faces of the young Africans than you'll see in some of the places of greatest privilege in America.

Dr. Robert Coles, a professor and research psychiatrist for Harvard University Health Services, said of his own academic setting, "We have systems here to explain everything—except how to live."[6] Philip Yancey, in his book *Soul Survivor,* devotes a chapter to the work of Dr. Coles among the poor. He writes,

Among the poor, he had expected defeat and despair; he found some, yes, but he also found strength and hope and courage. Among the rich he expected satisfaction, and instead found boredom, alienation, and decadence. . . . Comfortable people, he noticed, were apt to have a stunted sense of compassion. . . . Ultimately, he came to believe that the most dangerous temptation

---

*Our Mission Feeding ministry at Life Outreach International is taking much-needed food to areas on the continent of Africa where war, famine, drought, and poverty have taken their toll on the people. Through this ministry, food factories in Mozambique and Angola provide enough food each month to feed more than 300,000 starving children, mothers, elderly people, and people with disabilities.

of all is the temptation of plenty. In the same breath, wealth curses what it blesses. Being privileged, Coles concluded, tends to stifle compassion, curtail community, and feed ambition. . . . He had discovered that the poor are mysteriously blessed and that the rich live in peril. He had learned that what matters most comes not from without—the circumstances of life—but from within, inside the heart of an individual man or woman or child.[7]

As you proceed through the pages of this book, it is my earnest prayer that you will find your life being transformed to the point where you begin to experience abundance of life regardless of your circumstances, challenges, or obstacles. If you will allow me to share what I have seen and experienced during the sixty years of my personal pilgrimage, I really believe you will begin to experience true prosperity.

A SCRIPTURAL CASE FOR PROSPERITY

Prosperity is a biblical concept. But in order to understand *true* prosperity, we must view it within its scriptural context. One of the best examples of true prosperity can be found in the apostle Paul's description of the generosity demonstrated by the Macedonian churches in response to the needs of the church in Jerusalem.

*Out of the most severe trial, **their overflowing joy**
and their extreme poverty **welled up in rich
generosity.** For I testify that they gave as much
as they were able, and **even beyond their ability.**
Entirely on their own, **they urgently pleaded
with us for the privilege of sharing.***

(2 CORINTHIANS 8:2-4, emphasis added)

Here we see a church that is materially poor yet prosperous. Why? Because they possessed a heart for giving
and sharing. They gave themselves first to the Lord,
then to their brothers and sisters in need, thus fulfilling
the great commandment: "You shall love the Lord your
God with all your heart, and with all your soul, and
with all your strength, and with all your mind; and
your neighbor as yourself" (Luke 10:27, NASB). When
you love God with all your heart, you will begin to love
your neighbor, and the outward expression of this relationship and commitment will be undeniable. You will
share your time with others. You will give of your means,
and you will utilize to God's glory and to the benefit of
others the talent God has given you.

*See that you also excel in this grace of giving. **I am
not commanding you, but I want to test the
sincerity of your love** by comparing it with the*

earnestness of others. For you know the grace of our
Lord Jesus Christ, that though he was rich, yet
for your sakes he became poor, so that you
through his poverty might become rich.

(2 CORINTHIANS 8:7-9, emphasis added)

Paul says that our generosity is a test of our love—for
God and for others. He challenges us to be like the
Macedonian believers and to follow Christ's example.
But in citing the example of Christ, he's not talking
about *things*. Jesus did not leave earthly possessions
behind when he left heaven, yet he was still rich. He
gave his life for us that we might have abundant life,
and that in having it, we would allow it to be seen and
experienced by others.

Each man should give what he has decided in
his heart to give, **not reluctantly or under**
compulsion, *for God loves a cheerful giver. And*
God is able to make all grace abound to you, so
that in all things at all times, having all that you
need, you will abound in every good work.

(2 CORINTHIANS 9:7-8, emphasis added)

An essential part of experiencing and living in true
prosperity is learned through giving to others and to

God's purposes with a glad spirit—a cheerful heart. We look for places to sow good seed. We look for good soil. We don't focus our attention on the expected harvest, although we know it will come in due season. Our joy comes through the act of giving—giving of our time, our talent, our wisdom, our finances, and every good thing that comes from the Father above.

> *Now he who supplies seed to the sower and bread for food will also supply and increase your store of seed and will enlarge the harvest of your righteousness.* **You will be made rich in every way** *so that you can be generous on every occasion, and through us* **your generosity will result in thanksgiving to God.** *This service that you perform is not only supplying the needs of God's people but is also* ***overflowing in many expressions of thanks to God.*** (2 CORINTHIANS 9:10-12, emphasis added)

In this harvest of righteousness, be assured that it is God's righteousness enlarged in us, not our own self-righteousness, that will bear fruit. Paul tells us that we have been given wealth so that we can be continually generous. The purpose of prosperity is not so that we can sit back and enjoy the gifts God has given us; it is so that we can use these gifts to help reach a lost and dying world. Our generosity will result in thanksgiving to God. When we are generous with our resources, Paul assures us that we not only supply the needs of God's people, our sisters and brothers in Christ, but we also express our gratitude to God for the blessings he has bestowed on us.

> Our grounding in biblical truth has granted us opportunity, wisdom, privilege, and even the ability to gain wealth. We have been blessed beyond measure.

THE PURPOSE OF PROSPERITY

During Bill Clinton's presidency, an income tax increase was characterized as "a tax on the rich." Once the increase went into effect and millions of middle-class Americans saw their taxes go up, some political commentators and satirists joked, "It's a tax only on the rich . . . but guess what? You're rich!"

Although most middle-class Americans do not consider themselves "rich" or "wealthy," the very fact that they have food in their pantries, clothes in their closets, and a roof over their heads illustrates that their basic needs are met. The vast majority of Americans, and most citizens of other developed nations, including some who would be considered lower class in their societies, are, in the most basic sense, prosperous. They aren't skipping meals for lack of money. They have more than one change of clothes. They haven't slept out in the rain because they have no shelter. When you consider that an estimated 1.3 billion people—almost 25 percent of the world's population—subsist on less than one dollar per day, those of us who spend a dollar a day on unnecessary items would have to be considered well-off. In a very real sense, the pundits were right: You *are* rich.

Our nation was founded in part on Christian principles. Throughout most of our history, our society has reflected a strong commitment to Christian values. Because of this, we have prospered materially. Our grounding in biblical truth has granted us opportunity, wisdom, privilege, and even the ability to gain wealth. We have been blessed beyond measure.

The prophet Jeremiah, in a great passage about restoration, spoke of a similar outpouring of blessing on God's people, the tribes of Judah and Israel:

> *I will heal my people and will let them enjoy abundant peace and security. I will bring Judah and Israel back from captivity and will rebuild them as they were before. I will cleanse them from all the sin they have committed against me and will forgive all their sins of rebellion against me. Then this city will bring me renown, joy, praise and honor before all*

*nations on earth that hear of all the good things I do
for it; and they will be in awe and will tremble at
the abundant prosperity and peace I provide for it.*
JEREMIAH 33:6-9

In the New Testament Jesus tells us not to worry about
things like food and clothing but rather to focus on
seeking the Kingdom of God and his righteousness in
our lives (see Matthew 6:25-34). When we put our trust
completely in God and make his priorities our priorities, he promises to meet our needs. Christians in our
country and around the world have experienced the fulfillment of this promise. Those parts of the world that
reject Christ or embrace other gods have not experienced the fulfillment of this promise. It is no coinci-
dence, for example, that the least prosperous and most
tumultuous nation in the Western Hemisphere is Haiti,
a country founded on a pact with voodoo gods. God
has graciously given peace and prosperity to the United
States, Canada, and other nations with a strong Christian heritage. Most Christians recognize this fact and
thank God for it. However, with such blessing comes
great responsibility. As individuals and nations we
prosper so that we can help others. When we help others, the door opens to share the truth of Jesus Christ.
As we receive God's blessing, we pour it out on a lost

and dying world so that everyone may see God's blessing and come to know him. This three-part solution to the world's suffering, both physically and spiritually, represents the complete gospel.

He [Jesus] went to Nazareth, where he had been brought up, and on the Sabbath day he went into the synagogue, as was his custom. And he stood up to read. The scroll of the prophet Isaiah was handed to him. Unrolling it, he found the place where it is written: "The Spirit of the Lord is on me, because he has anointed me to preach good news to the poor. He has sent me to proclaim freedom for the prisoners and recovery of sight for the blind, to release the oppressed, to proclaim the year of the Lord's favor."

Then he rolled up the scroll, gave it back to the attendant and sat down. The eyes of everyone in the synagogue were fastened on him, and he began by saying to them, "Today this scripture is fulfilled in your hearing." (LUKE 4:16-21)

The Lord's favor has come to our world through Jesus Christ, and many of us have received his blessings. Now we must take the gospel to others by focusing on *their* needs, not *our* desires, and meeting them in any way possible. We should not be content to rest in our prosperity while much of the world suffers. It is our responsibility to help feed the hungry, give water to the thirsty, clothe the naked, and share the love of Jesus Christ. That is the purpose of our prosperity.

When you finish this book, make a gift of time, thoughtfulness, and money to a worthy cause—one that fulfills God's Kingdom purpose.

> *"Bring the whole tithe into the storehouse, so that there may be food in My house, and test Me now in this," says the Lord of hosts, "if I will not open for you the windows of heaven, and pour out for you a blessing until it overflows. Then I will rebuke the devourer for you, so that it may not destroy the fruits of the ground; nor will your vine in the field cast its grapes," says the Lord of hosts. "And all the nations will call you blessed, for you shall be a delightful land," says the Lord of hosts.*
>
> (MALACHI 3:10-12, NASB)

God says, "Test me in this," which means "trust me totally." He promises to rebuke the devourer and bless us with an overflowing abundance. This abundance, then, enables us to freely bless others. Verse 12 implies that others will notice the blessing of God on us and see us as a "delightful land." The New Testament tells us that the Holy Spirit enables us to express love, joy, peace, patience, and other good fruit of righteousness.

Sow in good soil with no thought of return. Trust God exclusively. Give as an expression of your trust in God; give because your heart has been changed. Regardless of your frame of mind, trust God. Then and only then will you be able to truly prosper.

There is an old adage that drives much of our ministry's mission outreach: "Give a man a fish to feed him for a day. Teach him to fish to feed him for a lifetime." Like that hungry man, many shortsighted Christians pray for a financial blessing (a fish) when God may want to teach them wisdom or how to use their time or talents in ways that will benefit them far more throughout their lives than a simple, one-time infusion of cash.

> As you learn to give as freely as you have received, you will discover true prosperity and understand that the greatest blessings in life are found in blessing others.

Be assured that the blessings God pours out will far exceed any monetary standard of measure. You will abound in fullness of life, love, peace, and grace, and in the confident assurance that you have touched the lives of others in a positive way for all eternity. As you learn to give as freely as you have received (Matthew 10:8), you will discover true prosperity and understand the reality of what Jesus said: "It is more blessed to give than to receive" (Acts 20:35). The greatest blessings in life are found in blessing others. It is amazing how much joy we experience when our focus is on God and others rather than on ourselves. It is only when we give up our lives for Christ (see Matthew 16:25-27) and for his purpose that we really find fullness and meaning in this life.

One word of caution: Following Jesus with your whole heart is no guarantee that your life will be without pain, suffering, hardship, or even tragedy. However, you can stand on the absolute truth that the Lord is your shepherd, and he will never leave you or forsake you. He will anoint your head with oil in the presence of very real enemies while preparing a table of divine provision for you. He will comfort you even in death's darkest valley (see Psalm 23).

God pours out his blessings on us even in the midst of suffering and trials. He will lift your head and be the shoulder upon which you may safely lean. He is the shelter in the storm, the high tower, the mighty fortress, the shield, and the unshakable rock foundation upon which you can securely build your life (see Psalms 3, 18, 27, 28, 61, 91, 144).

You cannot know true prosperity without knowing

God intimately. "Draw near to God and He will draw near to you" (James 4:8, NASB). Then you will be on the path to true prosperity.

QUESTIONS & ANSWERS

Does God want us to prosper?

Beloved, I pray that you may prosper in all things and be in health, just as your soul prospers. For I rejoiced greatly when brethren came and testified of the truth that is in you, just as you walk in the truth. I have no greater joy than to hear that my children walk in truth. (3 JOHN 1:2-4, NKJV)

Certainly, God desires for us to be free from the bondage of poverty, sickness, torment, and the other curses of this fallen world. But his primary concern is with our eternal souls. In several modern Bible translations, the word *prosper* is rendered as "that all may go well with you." God wants all to go well with us—whether in sickness or in health, in peacetime or in war, in triumph or in tribulation, in wealth or in need. This model of prosperity is seen in the lives of Jesus' disciples, who prospered spiritually even though they were beaten or killed, and often lived with limited material resources. Through it all, their souls prospered, and they lived with

True prosperity is seen in the lives of Jesus' disciples, who prospered spiritually even though they were beaten or killed and often lived with limited material resources. Through it all, their souls prospered, and they lived with abiding inner peace.

abiding inner peace in spite of their physical challenges. Contentment in all circumstances, giving freely as we have freely received: this is God's definition of prosperity.

God's definition of prosperity is what matters, not ours. He promises to supply our needs but not necessarily our selfish desires. We will have clothes, but they may not be the latest designer fashions. We will have food, but it may be a simple bowl of soup. We will have shelter, but it may be a small home in a modest neighborhood. Our time on this earth is short, our wealth is fleeting, but our prosperous souls will live for eternity. Surely we should focus on internal, eternal prosperity and rest assured that God is focused on what is best for us. If we will delight ourselves in him, then and only then will he give us the desires of our hearts (see Psalm 37:4).

God withheld certain things in my life until I was ready to handle them properly. As I matured, he entrusted me with more material possessions, because I had learned how to not let them become idols. Still, he tests my heart frequently for idolatry. How does the loss of something I enjoy affect me? How do I handle difficult circumstances that cost me time or money that could otherwise be used for more enjoyable activities? Learning how to pass these tests in life has been richly rewarding. I can say with genuine gratitude that I have passed the tests even as I have watched things I once treasured totally disappear or be destroyed, even by natural causes.

Learn to pray, "God, meet my needs," not "God, meet my desires or expectations." We should pray for God to make us trustworthy.

Should Christians have the wealth of the world?
One well-known minister's Web site mocks those who do not aspire to monetary wealth by saying, "We believe that it is more spiritual to say, 'I don't need or desire much,' or 'My rewards will come when I get to heaven.' We are usually trying to be humble when we say these things, but this is not humility; it is actually sin."

But is it a sin to be content with little? The apostle Paul himself wrote, "If we have food and covering, with these we shall be content. But those who want to get rich fall into temptation and a snare and many foolish and harmful desires which plunge men into ruin and destruction" (1 Timothy 6:8-9, NASB). These are the two verses that lead up to an oft-quoted verse: "For the love of money is a root of all sorts of evil" (v. 10, NASB).

Paul also wrote, in his letter to the believers in Philippi, "I have learned to be content in whatever circumstances I am. I know how to get along with humble means, and I also know how to live in prosperity; in any and every circumstance I have learned the secret of being filled and going hungry, both of having abundance and suffering need" (Philippians 4:11-12, NASB). Again, these two verses precede a well-known verse: "I can do all things through Him who strengthens me" (v. 13, NASB).

Compare this attitude with what David writes in the book of Psalms:

> The wicked draw the sword and bend the bow
> to bring down the poor and needy,
>   to slay those whose ways are upright.
> But their swords will pierce their own hearts,
>   and their bows will be broken.
>
> Better the little that the righteous have
>   than the wealth of many wicked;

for the power of the wicked will be broken,
  but the Lord upholds the righteous.
  (PSALM 37:14-17)

The clear message throughout Scripture is that it is better to have just a little money and be on God's side than to have a lot of money and be apart from God. The real emphasis is on righteousness, which does not necessarily coincide with large amounts of money.

One idea popular among some "prosperity preachers" is that Scripture teaches the transfer of wealth from the wicked world into the pockets of Christians. One passage sometimes used to support this notion is found in Isaiah 45:3: "I will give you the treasures of darkness, riches stored in secret places, so that you may know that I am the Lord."

This verse sounds great in the middle of a sermon about getting rich. But when we examine the full context of the passage, we see that the Lord was speaking through Isaiah to Cyrus, the Persian king whom God planned to use to deliver the Israelites from Babylon, even though he was not a righteous man. In fact, if we read the next four verses, we understand that Cyrus did not even acknowledge God. Rather, Isaiah is informing Cyrus of the great victory he was about to experience so that the king would know that God ruled over all of the affairs of men:

> For the sake of Jacob my servant,
>   of Israel my chosen,
> I summon you by name
>   and bestow on you a title of honor,
>   though you do not acknowledge me.
> I am the Lord, and there is no other;
>   apart from me there is no God.
>   I will strengthen you, though you have not
>   acknowledged me,
> so that from the rising of the sun
>   to the place of its setting
> men may know there is none besides me.
>   I am the Lord, and there is no other.
> I form the light and create darkness,
>   I bring prosperity and create disaster;
>   I, the Lord, do all these things.   (ISAIAH 45:4-7)

God was certainly saying something, but was he saying that twenty-first-century Christians will be rich? No! He was saying that he is in charge. In the case of Cyrus, God used an ungodly ruler to free his people from slavery. Then, instead of giving the spoils to the Israelites and thereby making them rich, he let Cyrus keep it himself. God's desire for Cyrus was that he would know God, and he used money to get his attention. God's priority for his people was not that they would be rich but that they would be free from bondage.

Although Isaiah 45 does not support the idea of the "transfer of wealth," there is another passage that better supports such a notion. In Proverbs 13:18-23 the writer deals with several truths related to finances:

> *Poverty and shame will come to him who neglects discipline,*
> *But he who regards reproof will be honored.*
> *Desire realized is sweet to the soul,*
> *But it is an abomination to fools to turn away from evil.*
> *He who walks with wise men will be wise,*
> *But the companion of fools will suffer harm.*
> *Adversity pursues sinners,*
> *But the righteous will be rewarded with prosperity.*
> *A good man leaves an inheritance to his children's children,*
> *And the wealth of the sinner is stored up for the righteous.*
> *Abundant food is in the fallow ground of the poor,*
> *But it is swept away by injustice.* (NASB)

Here, we see the idea that the righteous "prosper," but this is not a reference to material gain apart from the eternal blessings from God above. A "good man leaves an inheritance" only if he has something to leave behind. This could indicate some level of wealth, although it could also refer to a good name or other legacy. The next phrase, "and the wealth of the sinner is stored up for the righteous," provides the cornerstone of many misguided messages. Many scholarly commentators suggest that this is a reference to the Israelites obtaining the wealth of the Egyptians.

> In the church we often see two extreme views. One says that Christians should have nothing; the other says that Christians should have it all. Somewhere, a biblical balance must be found.

Similarly, Proverbs 28:8 seems to support the idea of ill-gotten gain ending up in the hands of the merciful: "He who increases his wealth by interest and usury gathers it for him who is gracious to the poor" (NASB), but the theme of this passage actually centers around the fleetingness of riches, especially when obtained immorally. God has a way of taking care of the poor, sometimes using the wealth of the wicked to do so. There is no evidence that it is God's desire to make all Christians rich by fleecing wealthy unbelievers. Instead, the message to be proclaimed is that money cannot replace the righteousness of God.

We can, however, receive wisdom and direction from God that may lead to financial success in this life. Divine inspiration and insight can lead to sound business investments, creative and inventive ideas, effective leadership, and wealth-producing decisions.

In the church we often see two extreme views. One says that Christians should have nothing; the other says that Christians should have it all. Somewhere, a biblical balance must be found. It's not about gaining monetary wealth; it's about learning to live with true prosperity and understanding what that actually means.

The reality is that some Christians possess great material wealth, while others possess little. God wants us to use our resources wisely, whatever their measure. He also wants us to be content with his provision, whether great or small, and avoid covetousness, which is the greedy desire to obtain other people's possessions. He wants us to trust him for our provision, whether we are rich or poor. And he wants us to gladly and faithfully give our finances to help others, whether it is a million dollars or a widow's mite.

CHAPTER 2

WHAT IS *NOT* TRUE PROSPERITY?

Much of what we learn in life comes via *negative* examples or by looking at contrasts or opposites. For instance, if I were describing a particular type of animal and I said, "Well, it doesn't fly, and it doesn't walk on two legs," you would be able to rule out most birds, primates, and many other animals. You wouldn't necessarily know if it was a fish or a snake, but you would be nearer to the correct answer by knowing the characteristics you could eliminate. Accordingly, we can learn a lot about true prosperity by studying what true prosperity is *not*. By stripping away misunderstandings related to prosperity, we can get down to the reality of the prosperous life. By tearing down the lies, we can build upon the truth. Then we will be able to pursue prosperity in the proper way.

There are many definitions of prosperity that are simply wrong. *Wealth, power, fame, recognition,* and *comfort* are perhaps the most popular misconceptions. Although these conditions may be part of a prosperous person's life, in and of themselves they are not an indication of true prosperity.

WEALTH

True prosperity is not merely the accumulation of material possessions or wealth. If it were, then only the righteous would be rich and the wicked would fall into poverty. But that's not how it works. All you have to do is study history or look around you to see that totally self-centered people can amass great monetary wealth. Some of the richest people in the world are also some of the most perverse, secretive, prideful, covetous, and greedy individuals ever to walk the earth. Yet, if we believe that such people cannot truly prosper, then there must be more to prosperity than simply having a lot of cash in the bank. Here's what the Bible says:

> *This is what the wicked are like—*
> *always carefree, they increase in wealth.*
> (PSALM 73:12)

A man of perverse heart does not prosper;
   he whose tongue is deceitful falls into trouble.
(PROVERBS 17:20)

He who conceals his sins does not prosper,
   but whoever confesses and renounces them finds
      mercy. (PROVERBS 28:13)

Here we see three traits of the wicked or self-absorbed. They have perverse hearts, they conceal their sins, and they increase in wealth. Therefore, monetary wealth alone cannot be a scriptural definition of prosperity. Although God often blesses believers with great material wealth, it is not necessarily a sign of spiritual depth or faith. In fact, Satan used material wealth and power to tempt Jesus Christ, claiming that he had the ability to give wealth (see Matthew 4:8-9).

POWER

Material wealth and power often go hand in hand. Some people would look at those in positions of power—politicians, businesspeople, cultural icons—and consider them prosperous. More than simply having money, these people also have the ability to influence world events, cultural trends, and people's lives. The president of the United States, for example, wields enormous power and influence, as do many business executives or celebrities such as Oprah Winfrey, whose recommended reading list can catapult a book onto the national best-sellers lists. These people have power, but does that make them prosperous?

Consider some others who had great power and lost it—people such as Adolf Hitler and Saddam Hussein. They used their power for evil purposes and had it stripped away violently. Power can be either a blessing or a curse, but in and of itself it is not a sign of true prosperity.

FAME

Like those in power, people who are well known are often considered to be prosperous. Athletes, artists, and even ordinary people who find themselves vaulted into the public eye due to extraordinary circumstances or events all find a measure of fame. Many people find they don't like the spotlight, whereas others revel in it.

As an evangelist and as a Christian leader, I have known many famous people, from football players to actors to preachers to politicians. Many of them have confided in me concerning their misery, their mistakes, and their loneliness. How about well-known artists and entertainers such as Ernest Hemingway, Marilyn Monroe, and Kurt Cobain? All were very successful in their respective artistic fields, yet all died at their own hand. In reality, fame is often a barrier to prosperity. It does not have to be that way, but too often it is. Some of the most oppressed, beaten down, and depressed people I have ever known are outwardly successful and famous.

You can have both fame and prosperity, or you can have one without the other, but fame and prosperity are certainly not the same thing.

RECOGNITION

Many people feel as if they would be happy if someone would just notice them. Whether it is winning an Academy Award or getting a promotion at work, almost everyone wants a little recognition at some point in their lives. But is it possible to be completely unnoticed, yet still prosperous? Recognition is nice, but prosperity does not come through the adoration or accolades of others.

Gaining recognition in the world does not guarantee prosperity. It might increase your status, your wealth, your influence, or your responsibilities, but it does not automatically instill inner peace and satisfaction. In fact, some of the most prosperous people in the world, in the true sense, are the least recognized. Jesus said, "Whoever wants to become great among you must be your servant" (Matthew 20:26). Servants don't get much recognition, but through their service they have a positive impact on the lives of others. Parents often don't get recognition, but their reward comes through the meaningful and productive lives of their children. Missionaries often toil in complete obscurity, yet their reward comes through the souls they reach with the gospel of Jesus Christ. The heart of a servant captures the essence of true prosperity.

COMFORT

Some people consider themselves prosperous because they have a big house, a nice car, a well-paying job, a functional family, and all the amenities of the American Dream. Indeed, some may be satisfied with a modest apartment and an enjoyable job because they feel as if they have everything they need. Although contentment is a part of true prosperity, mere comfort is not. In fact, comfort can be the enemy of prosperity because it can lull us into complacency. In the Old Testament, God's people were rebuked for being "at ease in Zion" (Amos 6:1, NASB).

In contrast, some of the more prosperous individuals portrayed in the Bible are people who suffered. The apostle Paul was in prison, for example, far from comfort, yet he considered himself so prosperous and free that he and his traveling companion, Silas, sang praises to God in the Philippian jail (see Acts 16:23-25). The prophet Elijah lived in a cave and had his food brought to him by birds, yet he prospered in his relationship with God. Comfort can be nice, but the inner peace of true prosperity, which comes by God's grace, is much better.

QUESTIONS & ANSWERS

Is wealth a sign of great faith?

Some teachers of the so-called prosperity gospel state explicitly—or strongly imply—that our financial status corresponds directly to our faith in God, as if material possessions equal spiritual depth. If we lack money, we must lack faith. If we gave money to their ministry and did not reap a financial reward, we have failed in our faith. They imply that spiritual faith always produces material gain. But few ideas could be farther from the truth.

Contrast this philosophy with the following verse: "This is what the wicked are like—always carefree, they increase in wealth" (Psalm 73:12). Although the psalmist does not categorically state that *only* the wicked increase in wealth, he does seem to rule out gauging the quality of our spiritual lives by our degree of material wealth. In other words, if the wicked can be wealthy, then we cannot automatically assume that a person of great wealth is a person of great faith. In fact, when we look at the heroes of faith depicted in Hebrews 11, we see that these models of true prosperity, including Abraham, Noah, Moses, and others, were not characterized as "rich." Instead, it says, "They went about in sheepskins and goatskins, destitute, persecuted and mistreated. . . . They wandered in deserts and mountains, and in caves and holes in the ground" (vv. 37-38). This description hardly aligns with a theology that says the faithful will have large homes, fancy cars, and expensive clothes.

In his research, Dr. Robert Coles observed that the poor often experience more peace and meaning in life than the privileged. I have observed this same phenomenon many times on mission fields around the world. Among villagers and families that have little or no material possessions, there is often more harmony, and the children laugh more freely, share more willingly, and experience life more fully than many people in affluent Western nations. Many poor people are, in fact, more prosperous than many who have great wealth.

Betty and I have been greatly blessed, sometimes even monetarily, because of the guidance God has given us in the decisions we have made. Although we have always lived below our means, even in meager times we have had nice things—which we enjoy. But these things do not give us the joy we have in our daily lives. Even the loss of these things does not take away our joy, because things are not the source of our prosperity or our happiness.

It is not necessary to take a vow of poverty in order to have abundant life. I must repeat: Possessing things is not the issue. It is when our things possess us and thereby replace spiritual reality and the relationship we can experience with God that they become a problem. Discovering the supernatural enabling to live with material wealth and still hold fast to the faith may be one of life's greatest achievements.

> It is not necessary to take a vow of poverty in order to have abundant life. Possessing things is not the issue. It is when our things possess us that they become a problem.

Years ago, after hearing and seeing how much people who faced great loss seemed to love God, I prayed, "Lord, why don't you take everything away from me, so that I can love you more?" He spoke to my heart, saying, "Why? So you will love me more than *nothing*? No, James, I'm going to bless you greatly so that you can love me more than *everything!*" That is the real

41

test—loving God more than everything, instead of loving him more than nothing.

The fact that so many great people of faith sold all their earthly possessions in an attempt to experience all that God can offer is a testimony to the power of material things and their potential to distract us. When Jesus asked, "What will it profit a man if he gains the whole world, and loses his own soul?" (Mark 8:36, NKJV), he was referring to far more than eternity. He was referring also to the present—the here and now on this earth. Many who claim salvation in Christ have actually received the great gift of grace—yet, in a way, they lose their soul: their joy, their peace, and their fullness of life.

Blessing in life comes through blessing others. When we bless others, we experience blessing at its highest level. The most important question is not, Can we live with joy and peace without an abundance of things? but *Can we actually live with joy and peace while having an abundance of possessions?*

Jesus left everything he possessed for our sake; yet, he also returned to it all and is presently seated at the right hand of the Father. The biblical truth is this: Material things are temporal, but spiritual things are eternal. To elevate our temporary circumstances above our eternal condition cheapens the things that are important to

God. Faith is far more important than riches. We need to set our minds on things above and stop focusing on the things that will pass away.

The more we focus on God, the more we will notice the needs of others and the more we will seek to meet those needs. In the process we will find our own lives blessed beyond measure.

In Luke 16 Jesus tells the parable about a rich man and a beggar. In this story, the beggar lived outside the gate of the rich man, "longing to eat what fell from the rich man's table." After both men died, the rich man found torment in hell, while the beggar found eternal comfort by the side of Abraham. Why did Jesus set these two men in contrast to each other, both in this life and in the afterlife? Consider his audience: the Pharisees. They were a group of wealthy religious leaders, described as "lovers of money." Many of them had turned the Temple into a marketplace. They were full of pride and looked down on those who did not have material wealth. Certainly they believed that the righteous would prosper and the wicked would suffer. The poor man's suffering appeared to them to be a result of his sin. Yet it was the beggar who ended up in heaven and the rich man who ended up in hell, begging for a drop of water.

Peter Pretorius, a missionary who feeds starving

people across the continent of Africa, says, regarding our giving to feed the hungry, "We are not measured by how much we give to others, but rather how much we keep for ourselves." When others' needs outweigh our own desires, we understand the heart of God. Our faith would then be demonstrated by how much we help those in need, not by how much we own.

The desire to own, build, develop, and enjoy our possessions is not the problem. Instead, it is our failure to leave the "corners of our cultivated fields" to the poor, as was the tradition in ancient agrarian times. It is our self-absorbed living, with no Good Samaritan deeds on behalf of the poor and the suffering, that reveals the hardness of our hearts and our lack of true prosperity.

Was Jesus a rich man?
A cornerstone principle of some "prosperity preachers" is that Jesus was a rich man (thus, by extension, we should be rich, as well).

Three pieces of evidence are commonly offered to support this claim. First, Jesus wore a "seamless" garment (John 19:23). Because this type of garment signified wealth—or so the argument goes—Jesus must have been rich. However, this explanation does not take into account the possibility that someone had given the seamless garment to Jesus as a gift, just as Mary poured out expensive perfume on Jesus' feet as an act of worship. Certainly, there were people of means who became followers of Jesus. Perhaps one of them honored the Lord by giving him the seamless garment.

Second, some people have argued that because Judas, the treasurer of Christ's disciples, stole from the treasury and nobody seemed to notice, their group must have had a lot of money. However, this belief is based on circumstantial evidence at best. Assigning financial responsibility to one person within a group may indicate organizational structure but not necessarily wealth. Even if that individual has the opportunity to "skim" a little off the top, it doesn't mean there's an abundance to be skimmed. It could be argued that Judas stole from the common purse precisely because the group did not have an abundance of money; otherwise, they would all be so rich that there would be no need to steal. There is no real evidence of wealth in the fact that Judas held the title of treasurer.

After Jesus' crucifixion, resurrection, and ascension, Peter and John claimed to have no money at all when asked by a crippled beggar outside the Temple gate. "Silver or gold I do not have," Peter said, "but what I have I give you. In the name of Jesus Christ of Nazareth, walk" (Acts 3:6). The man was instantly healed. Certainly that meant more to the man than all the money in the world, but it also raises an interesting question: If Jesus had been rich and the twelve disciples had had a lot of money, wouldn't Peter and John have had a few pennies to spare for the beggar? Surely they were not lying about their financial condition.

The third argument made by some preachers is that poverty is a sin—and because Jesus was sinless, he must have been rich. This explanation stretches common sense quite a bit. Certainly one can have his or her basic needs met—thereby avoiding poverty—without having excessive riches.

The counterarguments to the belief that Jesus was wealthy—the points most often noted by those claiming he was financially poor—lie in three passages of Scripture, two of which are parallel.

The first two verses, Matthew 8:20 and Luke 9:58, both contain accounts of Jesus saying, "Foxes have holes and birds of the air have nests, but the Son of Man has no place to lay his head." Some teachers assert that this statement proves that Jesus was homeless, but the context is rather that Jesus is calling people to follow him, and he is explaining the cost of discipleship. He knew that he would be traveling, teaching, and preaching. He knew of his impending crucifixion. This verse most likely serves as a warning to his followers that life would not be easy for them. Indeed, many of his disciples lived difficult lives.

Even today, many people choose to follow Christ at great risk to their welfare, reputation, possessions, and even their very lives. Betty and I have closely observed many missionaries who live sacrificially yet experience overwhelming joy and peace while also facing monumental challenges.

The third verse often cited is 2 Corinthians 8:9: "For you know the grace of our Lord Jesus Christ, that though he was rich, yet for your sakes he became poor, so that you through his poverty might become rich." If we understand this verse as a reference to monetary riches, it could actually be used to advance both the "Jesus was a rich man" and "Jesus was a poor man" arguments. If Jesus were rich but became poor, which example are we to follow? The one who was rich or the one who voluntarily became poor?

Many Bible scholars note that Jesus, upon leaving

> Many people choose to follow Christ at great risk to their welfare, reputation, possessions, and even their very lives. Many missionaries live sacrificially yet experience overwhelming joy and peace while also facing monumental challenges.

his seat at the throne of God the Father to take the lowly form of a man, became "poor" in that he became one of us. And because of this sacrifice on our behalf, we are able, through the power of the Resurrection, to reestablish a relationship with God the Father, thereby becoming "rich," as it says in 2 Corinthians 8:9. Tying the awesome concept of grace strictly to monetary values demeans the reality of the heavenly abundance now available to us through the sacrifice of Jesus Christ.

In balance, there really is not enough evidence to suggest that Jesus, as a man walking the earth, lived at either extreme—in poverty or in great wealth. The balance of biblical evidence suggests that his basic needs were met and fine gifts were given to him, but he did not value the accumulation of large amounts of money or material possessions. Certainly he was (and is) rich beyond measure in that "the earth is the Lord's, and everything in it" (Psalm 24:1) and he owns "the cattle on a thousand hills" (Psalm 50:10), yet he sought to go beyond earthly riches and press us to focus on more important riches—the wealth of the human soul and the abundant life in Christ available to us both in heaven and on earth. The more important lesson we learn about riches from examining the life of Christ is this: It's not about getting rich—it's about living richly.

Why do people get rich by preaching a false prosperity message?

When a person preaches a "gospel" of greed and covetousness, how is it possible for them to reap such a bountiful reward? The answer is actually quite simple. In fact, the same old scheme pops up every few years in different areas of the country under different names. One of the recent incarnations of this ruse (known as a Ponzi scheme or a pyramid scheme) appeared under the name The Friends Network. This plan required new recruits to send a "gift" of $1,000 to a "friend" already in the network. Then the new "friend" would enlist two or three additional "friends" to give back into the network. People all over the country were getting rich in just a few weeks! Of course, the law forbids such pyramid schemes, and law enforcement officials shut down these networks as quickly as possible, but inevitably the people at the top of the pyramid—the founders of the network—make money fast. In the process, those nearest the top of the pyramid provide wonderful testimonials, which serve to encourage new people to join, thus expanding the pyramid exponentially. The laws of mathematics eventually determine that those in the upper echelon of the pyramid benefit, while those at the bottom lose.

Similarly, when a preacher comes along promising

When a preacher comes along promising great financial reward to people who will give to the preacher's ministry, the pyramid principle operates to make those at the top wealthy.

great financial reward to people who will give to the preacher's ministry and to other believers in the system, the pyramid principle operates to make those at the top wealthy. Great testimonials abound as those at the top point to their own burgeoning wealth as evidence of the efficacy of what they are preaching. Consequently, more and more people are motivated to participate. The inevitable backlash of the pyramid scheme is diffused by providing spiritual explanations to excuse the lack of reward for those at the bottom of the pyramid—things such as "you just lacked faith" or "you didn't pray correctly"—which allows the pyramid to continue to build.

Most preachers do not intentionally engage in pyramid schemes. Some truly believe that they deserve to get rich by pushing the prosperity message. But the laws of mathematics operate regardless of motivation, and in the process, large numbers of people lose money by being on the wrong end of the deal.

Be assured that anyone who engages in a religious Ponzi scheme will not experience true prosperity. They may profit financially in the short term, but the abundance of God is not with them. True prosperity encompasses so much more than merely money. It includes having the time, the talent, the wisdom, and the wealth of God—as well as his presence, which allows us to use our God-given resources for his purposes, not our own.

CHAPTER 3

KEYS TO TRUE PROSPERITY

IF TRUE prosperity is not found in material wealth, power, fame, recognition, or comfort, how can we become truly prosperous? Although prosperity ultimately comes from God, there are several things we can do to position ourselves for God's release of blessing in our lives.

In discussing these keys to true prosperity, however, we must understand that the motivation for pursuing these avenues of blessing cannot be purely self-serving. Our focus must be on obedience to God and his Word, not on the expected benefits. We must seek with all of our hearts to live in God's will.

KEY #1: WALK RIGHTEOUSLY

The way we conduct our daily lives lays much of the foundation for prosperous living. Isaiah 33:14-16 wonderfully illustrates this truth:

> *The sinners in Zion are terrified;*
> *trembling grips the godless:*
> *"Who of us can dwell with the consuming fire?*
> *Who of us can dwell with everlasting burning?"*

When the people of God—those in Zion—are really not living in faith and not living in the absolute truths of prosperity, they become terrified and face pressures and temptations that become a "consuming fire." When this pressure comes, there is only one proper response:

> *He who walks righteously*
> *and speaks what is right,*
> *who rejects gain from extortion*
> *and keeps his hand from accepting bribes,*
> *who stops his ears against plots of murder*
> *and shuts his eyes against contemplating evil—*
> *this is the man who will dwell on the heights,*
> *whose refuge will be the mountain fortress.*
> *His bread will be supplied,*
> *and water will not fail him.*

The ones who will experience true prosperity are those who walk in God's righteousness (not their own), speak sincerely, tell the truth, reject selfish and unjust gain, refuse to take bribes, and don't compromise their God-given convictions. This is the essence of righteous living. Be warned, however, that when we actually walk in righteousness, we are only one misstep away from judgmental, critical self-righteousness. "Pride goes before destruction, a haughty spirit before a fall. Better to be lowly in spirit and among the oppressed than to share plunder with the proud. Whoever gives heed to instruction prospers, and blessed is he who trusts in the Lord" (Proverbs 16:18-20). "So, if you think you are standing firm, be careful that you don't fall!" (1 Corinthians 10:12).

The blessed person stops his ears from hearing about bloodshed or destruction, does not look upon evil, yet never becomes critical, arrogant, or self-righteous. And we must make certain that in our refusal to compromise we don't also refuse to love or forgive. Only the merciful will themselves obtain mercy (see Matthew 5:7).

Those who "dwell on the heights" are able to see far off. They have excellent long-term vision. Their refuge is an impregnable rock. They are unshakable because they are walking on the solid rock of hearing and *doing* the truth. If we walk righteously, God says, our needs will always be met. This is true prosperity.

KEY #2: BECOME A GIVER

> *Give, and it will be given to you. A good measure, pressed down, shaken together and running over, will be poured into your lap. For with the measure you use, it will be measured to you.* (LUKE 6:38)

Anyone who has been around the church for any length of time has heard Luke 6:38 quoted. But too often the focus is wrongly placed on the latter part of the first sentence: *"It will be given to you."*

The lesson here is not that God wants his people to learn how to *get*. The Western mentality that asks, "What's in it for me?" has carried over into ministry. "All right, Pastor, if I get right with God, if I give to the offering, if I become a giver, what's in it for me?" If this is the motivation behind our giving, then we have missed the point entirely. Our motivation should be obedience to God and a loving desire to bless the Lord and other people with the resources that God has entrusted to us. Learning to deny ourselves in order to help others is a vital step toward a meaningful life.

Our thoughts should not be on the return but on

releasing blessing and provision to the glory of God and the good of other people. Ironically, focusing on the return seems to be the most effective way to block God's blessing in our lives, because typically our expectations are not the same as God's promise. For example, if a woman begins to honor God by giving her time to the church, yet stays focused on her bank account for a financial reward, she may completely miss it when the Lord introduces her to a friend who can impart priceless wisdom into her life. Because she is focused on the wrong return, she may conclude that her service to the church is pointless. In truth, the friendship may be worth far more than a few dollars and could, in fact, lead her in a direction that would eventually benefit her financially. The point is that although God's blessings are promised, they are not to be our priority. Our motivation in every aspect of life must be love, obedience, and compassion (see Philippians 2:1-13; Colossians 3:12-17).

On numerous occasions, including times when I had limited or meager financial resources, I helped someone who was facing seemingly impossible challenges. Later, when that person was blessed with financial gain, he or she sought me out to help our ministry bless others.

I am convinced that if you will take hold of this truth and your heart's focus changes, it will be impossible to stop God's blessing in return. God's nature is one of mercy, love, and blessing. The law of sowing and reaping is an absolute law, but we must leave the return up to the will and timing of the Lord.

The law of sowing and reaping is an absolute law, but we must leave the return up to the will and timing of the Lord.

Jesus said, "It is more blessed to give than to receive" (Acts 20:35). Throughout the Gospels, Jesus puts the primary focus on the joy of giving, not on the return. He offers us the supreme example of what it means to give, in that he gave his life for us, even though he knew there was nothing we could give him in return. He knew that some would respond to him, that the return would be people coming to him in faith. Jesus knew that by giving his life, he would gain many children for his Father—and he has. But his gift of love was for our sake, for our gain, not his own.

Many ministers who use Luke 6:38 as their primary text—"Give, and it will be given to you"—seem to overlook a previous verse (v. 35) that emphasizes the importance of doing good, even lending, *without expecting to get anything back*" (italics added). Imagine a preacher standing in front of a crowd and asking for a "vow" or "seed money," then telling those who give to expect *nothing* in return! Yet this is essentially what Jesus Christ, the greatest teacher of all, the very embodiment of truth itself, said. Why? Because he came to give for the benefit of others. He established the principle that *giving is living.*

Remember the story of the Good Samaritan who helped the injured man at the side of the road (see Luke 10:30-37)? He didn't put oil on the injured man's wounds hoping to suddenly inherit an oil well. He didn't pay for the man's care at the local inn because he thought he would be rewarded with his own resort hotel. He came to the man's aid because the love of God flowed out of him freely. He was the true good neighbor that Christ says we're to emulate.

Jesus' concern for the poor and the outcast is one of the most common themes in the Gospel of Luke. The reference in Luke 6:38 to "good measure, pressed down, shaken together and running over" harkens back to the days when people would go to the marketplace for grain. The grain was poured out, shaken down, and filled to overflowing so that the buyer would receive the amount paid for. Although we know that we "reap what we sow," Jesus was not necessarily promising a return of our gift in kind but rather an equivalent return in joy and blessing. The point here is that those who give generously will be blessed generously. God won't shortchange a cheerful giver, but he gives intangible gifts as well as material blessings.

KEY #3: LOVE NOT THE WORLD

If your heart is set on the things of this world, you will chase after worldly gain instead of heavenly pursuits. Jesus cautions us: "Do not store up for yourselves treasures on earth, where moth and rust destroy, and where thieves break in and steal. But store up for yourselves treasures in heaven, where moth and rust do not destroy, and where thieves do not break in and steal" (Matthew 6:19-20). The reason that Jesus deals with worldly wealth so candidly is that he wants our hearts to be in the right place. He tells us, "Where your treasure is, there your heart will be also" (v. 21).

The fact is, where we invest our money says volumes about our desires and the focus of our hearts. Jesus says we cannot serve two masters: God on the one hand and "mammon"—which literally refers to money or riches—on the other. God wants us to put our trust completely in him. It is ironic that the words *In God We Trust* are printed on the back of our currency, because if we don't put our trust in God, we will undoubtedly put it in something else—and most likely that will be money.

Do not love the world or anything in the world. If anyone loves the world, the love of the Father is not in him. For everything in the world—the cravings of sinful man, the lust of his eyes and the boasting of what he has and does—comes not from the Father but from the world. The world and its desires pass away, but the man who does the will of God lives forever. (1 JOHN 2:15-17)

Does this admonition in Scripture mean you can't have a nice car? No! Just don't let the nice car have you. Does it mean you can't own a big house? No! Just don't let the big house own you. Do not allow the things of this world to take your heart captive. If you do, it is impossible to enjoy anything in this world. God also says that he "richly supplies us with all things to enjoy" (1 Timothy 6:17, NASB). Idols provide neither life nor joy—they rob us of both!

Wealth cannot be purchased with money; yet, money can often steal one's wealth. For some people, wealth becomes a source of fear because they are constantly worried that they may lose it or have it taken away.

Our trust must be exclusively in Jesus Christ. He is our provider in every way. Once we come to this understanding, we experience the freedom to give as he

For some people, wealth becomes a source of fear because they are constantly worried that they may lose it or have it taken away.

has given. If we know that we will lack for nothing, as he promises his children, then we can share his blessing without worry for ourselves. Truly the focus of "give and it shall be given unto you" is on the first word: *give*. God wants us to release every part of ourselves—our love, our time, our words, our money—for his Kingdom purpose. In not loving the world, we must learn how to live in the joy of giving (see Psalm 37:4; Philippians 4:19).

KEY #4: GLADLY BECOME A SERVANT

One of the fastest ways to find prosperity in our lives is to take on the role of a servant. If we truly assume the attitude and role of Jesus Christ by serving others in humility and grace, we will be truly prosperous in our souls and lives now.

When we seek to give more to others in every relationship, *we create an atmosphere for blessing.* In order to make serving our top priority, though, we must allow God's Spirit to begin developing in us the characteristics of Christ. A good servant is patient, kind, self-disciplined, and faithful. Living a Spirit-filled life is essential to godly service. We ask God to cleanse us from sin, selfishness, and every idol and fill us instead with the Holy Spirit.

The idea of servanthood as the means to prosperity is a complete paradigm shift from traditional strategies for success. True servants look out for the interest of others, not their own. True servants work to make others successful, not themselves. True servants rejoice in the triumphs of others, not just their own. And true servants always sacrifice themselves for their master.

James Anthony Froude, the great English historian, said, "Where all are selfish, the sage is no better than the fool, and only rather more dangerous." Selfish living makes people into dangerous, destructive fools. The surest way to avoid becoming such a fool is to embrace the role of a servant.

Jesus told his disciples, "Whoever wants to become great among you must be your servant" (Matthew 20:26). He knew that in order for any of us to succeed and truly prosper, we must willingly and joyously take on the role of a servant.

One of the things that influenced me greatly in the early days of both my ministry and my marriage was an encounter I had with a family in a church where I conducted a revival. This couple had four children and lived in a modest neighborhood not far from the church. What caught my attention was their little four-year-old daughter, who'd had her lower leg removed, just below the knee, in a battle with cancer.

I watched this beautiful little girl hobbling around on crutches, her face radiant with the warmest smile, and sensed an aura of peace enveloping the entire household. As the father held another child and watched the other two playing, the mother told me that she had once held a very good job. In fact, she had earned a larger salary than her husband. But as their family grew and their young daughter underwent treatment for cancer, they strongly believed that it was more important to spend time together as a family than to flourish financially. Even though it meant living on less than half of what they had once earned, this family had put their relationship with the Lord and with each other at the top of their priorities. They realized that the greatest service they could provide to their daughter and to the Lord was to give of their time to care for and love one another.

I remember sitting in their home, looking at a family that faced such a heartrending experience, and being astonished at such an atmosphere of peace and contentment. As a young man who was just about to establish a family of my own, I learned a valuable lesson in servanthood and witnessed firsthand what I now know as true prosperity.

Over the years I have witnessed the same joy and peace in couples and families out on the mission field, where they have left everything behind in order to seek God's purpose in their lives and in the lives of others. I have witnessed the same godly atmosphere in homes here in America, where people have discovered that life is not about *things;* it is about investing our lives to glorify and honor God.

I have also discovered that when people live according to eternal values yet find themselves blessed with temporal possessions, these things do not distract them from their true purpose and the true Source of life. Rather, when possessions are kept in their proper place, as resources to use in our service to Christ and other people, we also gain a measure of enjoyment in the use of these things, even as we serve.

KEY #5: ESCAPE THE BONDAGE OF DEBT

There can be no freedom or beauty about a life that depends on borrowing or debt. (Henrik Ibsen, *A Doll's House*)

Perhaps the greatest modern obstacle to "living in giving" is the problem of debt—not just a home mortgage or a regular car payment, but debt that becomes bondage. When personal debt prevents us from helping others, gladly giving to God, or making meaningful choices, we are in bondage. The materialistic mind-set of Western society promotes a "buy it now" mentality that can quickly create a financial prison. The irony in the United States is that even though there is no debtors' prison, millions of Americans live chained to their debt, unable to make clear-minded decisions, unable to truly rest at night, and unable to respond to God's prompting.

Christian counselors confirm that money—usually the lack thereof—is one of the most common wedges that come between husbands and wives, between parents and children, and between friends. Although money itself can strain a relationship, debt can bury it. The apostle Paul writes, "Give everyone what you owe him: If you owe taxes, pay taxes; if revenue, then revenue; if respect, then respect; if honor, then honor. *Let no debt remain outstanding,* except the continuing debt to love one another, for he who loves his fellowman has fulfilled the law" (Romans 13:7-8, italics added). Debt, specifically the type of debt that seeks to enslave, must not be a part of our lives if we wish to be everything that God wants us to be.

In times of national crisis, such as war in the Middle East, a disastrous hurricane, or other humanitarian crises within our borders, the government makes moves to stop a practice called price gouging. If an earthquake knocks out a city's water supply, for example, grocery stores in the area cannot double the price of bottled water. During the Gulf War, gas stations were penalized if their prices were too far above the going rate. For some reason, though, we don't apply the same emergency standards to our financial institutions. Even in times of recession, banks are allowed to charge double, triple, and up to four times the interest rate on such things as home loans, car loans, and the prime-lending rate for credit-card debt and other unsecured loans. The primary reason for this is that such loans are not leveraged against anything solid. Banks can charge exorbitant interest rates plus service fees, over-the-limit fees, late fees, and other penalties with no price-gouging laws to stop them. They solicit debtors through the mail with low-interest introductory offers; they conspire with other businesses to force us to carry their product (namely, a credit card); and they oftentimes show no mercy or consideration for the circumstances of a debtor's life. We may be allowed to skip payment on the principal, which would reduce our debt, but if we miss paying their interest—money that we will never see again and that benefits us in no way at all—we open ourselves up to regular harassment via telephone, increased interest rates, and, in some cases, veiled threats to be "turned over to collections," or worse. Credit cards are the greatest potential debt-bondage trap of our time. It is foolishness to enter into a contract to pay high interest on an unsecured loan. Credit-card debt is financial quicksand and must be avoided.

The Bible says that "the borrower is servant to the lender" (Proverbs 22:7). Why would we voluntarily enslave ourselves to lenders who, arguably, serve mammon and not God? It is clear that lending and borrowing are not wrong because in both the Old and New Testaments we're encouraged to lend in proper, constructive ways. The problem lies in debt bondage and the destructive pressure it puts on borrowers.

> **Credit-card debt is financial quicksand and must be avoided.**

Randy Alcorn, author of numerous books on finances and giving, writes in *Money, Possessions, and Eternity,* "Our self-centered, debt-centered economy is like those electronic bug-zappers. They emit a light attractive to insects that blissfully fly right into the trap, only to be killed."[8] A well-known investment advisor put it this way: "Nobody's ever gotten rich in this world getting money for 18 to 20 percent." Without a doubt, improper use of credit cards is one of the quickest and easiest ways to build up a mountain of debt.

The best rule for avoiding debt bondage is this: If you cannot afford it, don't buy it.

Let's face it, if you have cash, you don't need credit. If you legitimately need something—emphasis on *need,* not merely desire—then ask God for it. God promises to provide all of our needs, the things we need to take care of ourselves and our loved ones.

The best rule for avoiding debt bondage is this: If you cannot afford it, don't buy it. If you have cash, you don't need credit.

Need a way to get to work every day? Don't stretch yourself beyond your financial means. Ask God and let him work a miracle to get you to work. He may not supply a new BMW—it may be a used Ford. Or it may not be a car at all; it may be an opportunity to build a relationship with a coworker who lives nearby, so that he or she can provide you a ride to work and you can make a new friend and share the gospel. Trust God to supply all of your needs, and allow him to be God. We do not dictate the terms by which he answers our prayers, and we should not circumvent his will by getting ourselves into debt bondage trying to answer our own prayers.

Here are some obvious signs that indicate debt

bondage: rolling credit balances from one card to another; consistently coming up short on bill payments each month; lacking cash for unexpected expenses; or charging an item without knowing whether or not you will be able to pay for it.

If you are already in debt bondage, there are some things that you must do to get out. Before you pray and ask God to pull you out of your pit, whether it's self-created or dealt to you by circumstances, you must first check your own habits and practices. In the truest sense, sin is defined as "missing the mark." If you are in debt bondage, you have missed the mark. Repentance, the way out of sin, is simply "turning" or "changing direction." Therefore, to get out of debt, you must stop going in the direction that got you into debt and turn around. It may mean that you have to sell a car or your house, sacrifice unnecessary items, or seek immediate financial counseling. If managing money is not your strength, talk to someone who is qualified or gifted in that area. Obviously, the quickest way out of debt is to spend less and earn more. But please also

> To get out of debt, you must stop going in the direction that got you into debt and turn around. Obviously, the quickest way out of debt is to spend less and earn more.

consider consulting with a financial counselor—prefera-
bly a Christian—who can help you evaluate your own
unique situation and give you specific steps to put you
on the road to recovery.

One friend who has learned much about getting out
of debt through obedience to God is a businessman
from Alabama named Dan. I asked him to share his
story of obedience and prosperity, and he graciously
agreed. Here is Dan's story, which he calls "The Life
God Blesses":

As a young businessman, I learned some great lessons about the life
God blesses. I learned that blessings are not always financial and the
greatest blessings can never be bought. To me, nothing compares to
sitting on my back porch early in the morning and spending time with
my Creator, talking to him and hearing him talk to me, providing
instruction and direction for the day. Money cannot buy the blessing
of going on a long walk with my wife, listening and talking to her, or
spending time with our family and seeing the wonderful fruit that
comes from obeying God. I could go on and on about the many
blessings that money can't buy, yet as a young Christian I struggled
with the question of how to be blessed financially.

When I became a Christian, I had no job, no car, and no money.
When my wife and I got married, we were thrust into financial
blessings almost immediately. Within thirty days after the wedding,

I had a job that paid $750 for my first week of work, we had a house that we rented for only $45 per month, and we had two cars—one completely paid for and the other financed by my new employer.

Three years later my employer suddenly decided to shut down the business and sell all of his assets to pursue another business career. By this time, my wife and I were over $150,000 in debt. Facing this mountain of debt and now with no job, I began to seek God for direction. A good friend and I went on a three-day fast to separate ourselves from the distractions of everyday life and put ourselves in a position where we could hear God.

One night as I was praying, I sensed that God was leading me to start my own business. Yet, I was so far behind on my debts that my credit had been damaged to the point that no banks were interested in helping with the financing necessary to start my own business. I also had no experience or education in business. I was considered high risk! However, I kept seeking direction and help from God.

Ultimately, a local Christian businessman offered to help me get started. With faith and vision, I pressed forward with all my might to build a company that would bring glory to God, yet I found my financial debt load kept climbing. Eventually, I told my wife that I could not see how we could avoid filing bankruptcy. Working from early morning to midnight for a long, long time had finally caught up with me, and I had nothing else to offer.

As my wife and I discussed our situation, we agreed that unless God did a miracle we would have to file bankruptcy. We then decided to get on our knees and commit everything to the Lord. We told God that we had failed in our business, but if he could turn things around, we would dedicate the business to him and let it become a financial resource to fund his work around the world. We also did something else that I think was significant: We took full responsibility for our failure, and we did not blame God.

I must confess, I did not expect God to come through. The truth is, I had concluded that my business had failed and it was over. Little did I know that God had a different plan. The next morning an older Christian businessman contacted me and said that, during a prayer meeting the night before, he and a group of businessmen had taken up a collection to help me, and he wanted to teach me how to manage my business. The amount of their donation was just enough to allow me to make a small payment to each of my creditors, and the businessman helped me to arrange a payment plan with each of my creditors to pay them off over time.

Over the next four years, I sent small periodic payments to my creditors, along with a letter assuring them that I intended to pay them in full. At first, I sent $1 to $5 payments on $5,000 to $10,000 debts. For a long time it seemed I would never get these debts paid off, but eventually those checks went from $1 to $10 to $100 to $1,000, until one day we became debt-free. God is so good and always faithful!

During those four years of learning how to manage our business and our finances, God taught me some great principles.

"But seek first his kingdom and his righteousness, and all these things will be given to you as well" (Matthew 6:33).

The word *seek* means "to covet earnestly" and "to strive after." The word *strive* means "to contend, to struggle, wrestle, fight, to battle and engage in a conflict or contest." As I began to contend, struggle, wrestle, fight, battle, and engage in the conflict of discovering what it means to seek first the Kingdom of God, I heard an elderly preacher by the name of Clarence Matheny share a passage of Scripture that God used to bring a simple revelation that changed my life forever and unlocked financial blessings, as well as many other blessings that money could never buy:

"The kingdom of God is not a matter of eating and drinking, but of righteousness, peace and joy in the Holy Spirit" (Romans 14:17).

I began to see that my challenge as a Christian was to show the world the Kingdom of God by my lifestyle. I discovered that if I would seek to do what is right; walk in peace no matter what I faced; rejoice always, regardless of my trials and tribulations; and walk in the Holy Spirit, then all these other things—like money, houses, cars, and every other thing that people spend most of their time seeking—would become secondary.

I also discovered a major principle of God's Kingdom: increase according to the parable of the ten minas (a New Testament monetary unit), found in Luke 19:11-26. I learned that no matter how much or how little God entrusted to me, he wanted me to invest and use it faithfully for his Kingdom. Most important of all, I learned how to listen to God daily, to trust him, to seek to understand what he was saying, and to believe and obey whatever he said. I learned that if I would fight, struggle, wrestle, and battle to do God's will, and if I would endure hardship, suffering, and whatever else I had to face until the battle was over and the victory was won, I would finish whatever God had told me to do.

Clarence Matheny also taught me that faith comes when we hear God speak. He said we can know or discern that it is God speaking when we know God's written Word and can see how things he has promised in the past have come to fruition.

I later learned that there is a rest in God where we rest not *from* work but *in* work. It's a place where we cease from our own labor, and we become hidden in Christ; where we only do what he says, when he says to do it; where we become like Jesus, who didn't speak unless his Father told him what he should say.

These were key Scriptures and principles that God used in my journey. Because of God's faithfulness, we have found blessings beyond financial prosperity. To God be the glory!

This man and his wife have not only been blessed, they continually bless others; and in this they experience fullness of life.

QUESTIONS & ANSWERS

What does it mean to serve *mammon*?

No one can serve two masters; for either he will hate the one and love the other, or else he will be loyal to the one and despise the other. You cannot serve God and mammon. (MATTHEW 6:24, NKJV)

This oft-quoted verse contains an interesting and frequently misunderstood reference to a personality that stands in opposition to God. The New International Version states it this way: "No one can serve two masters. Either he will hate the one and love the other, or he will be devoted to the one and despise the other. You cannot serve both God and Money." Notice that the letter *M* is capitalized in *Money*. In English grammar this connotes a proper noun—a place, title, or person.

Mammon is a word that comes from Aramaic. It signifies personal gain or profit but not always monetarily. Although the word *mammon* in the Bible appears only in the Gospels, other Scripture passages refer to things that would qualify as "mammon," such as "the lust of the flesh, the lust of the eyes, and the pride of life" (1 John 2:16, NKJV). Some people serve their appetites; others serve pleasure, sleep, their place in society, or, of course, their wealth. These are all mammon. They are worldly, selfish, and in direct competition with God. God says, "Be content with what you have" (Hebrews 13:5). Mammon says, "Grab all you can." God says, "Act justly . . . love mercy . . . walk humbly" (Micah 6:8). Mammon says, "The end justifies the means." God says, "Give" (Luke 6:38). Mammon says, "Get." Though there's nothing wrong with using currency for exchanging goods and services, Mammon is a power that seeks to dominate us.

Immediately after Jesus tells us to guard against the demonic personality of Mammon (Matthew 6:24), he tells us not to be concerned about the material things of this world, even to the point of not worrying over our food, shelter, and clothing:

> *Therefore I tell you, do not worry about your life, what you will eat or drink; or about your body, what you will wear. Is not life more important than food, and the body more important than clothes? Look at the birds of the air; they do not sow or reap or store away in barns, and yet your heavenly Father feeds them. Are you not much more valuable than they? Who of you by worrying can add a single hour to his life? And why do you worry about clothes? See how the lilies of the field grow. They do not labor or spin.*

> *Yet I tell you that not even Solomon in all his*
> *splendor was dressed like one of these. If that is how*
> *God clothes the grass of the field, which is here today*
> *and tomorrow is thrown into the fire, will he not*
> *much more clothe you, O you of little faith? So do*
> *not worry, saying, "What shall we eat?" or "What*
> *shall we drink?" or "What shall we wear?" For the*
> *pagans run after all these things, and your heavenly*
> *Father knows that you need them. But seek first his*
> *kingdom and his righteousness, and all these things*
> *will be given to you as well. Therefore do not worry*
> *about tomorrow, for tomorrow will worry about*
> *itself. Each day has enough trouble of its own.*
> (MATTHEW 6:25-34)

Have you been wishing for a new car? Don't worry
about it! Do you want a bigger house? Don't worry
about it! Did you give money to a ministry, hoping to
get enough cash back to buy an expensive wardrobe?
Quit focusing on that! Instead, seek after God and his
Kingdom. Make this pursuit your only priority, because
you cannot serve God *and* your appetites. If you are
more concerned about material things than about the
righteousness of God, then you are serving mammon.
Repent, and pursue God.

Our pastor, Robert Morris, told Betty and me, "One

of our church members told me that he discovered that worry really does work. When I asked him what he meant by that, he said, 'Nothing I worry about ever happens, so worrying must work.'" Worry is such a waste of time. If you want true prosperity, stop worrying about material gain and focus your attention on pursuing the righteousness of God.

CHAPTER 4

WHAT SHOULD WE DO WITH OUR MONEY?

THE SCRIPTURES tell us several things to do with our money. Interestingly, none of them has to do with selfish motivations or fulfilling our own desires. Instead, they all deal in some fashion with helping and caring for others. For example, 2 Corinthians 9:6-15 expounds the law of sowing and reaping, encouraging believers to give bountifully and cheerfully. The passage makes it clear that God causes his grace to abound so that we may have the means to do good deeds on behalf of others: "He who supplies seed to the sower and bread for food will also supply and increase your store of seed and will enlarge the harvest of your righteousness" (v. 10).

Ephesians 4:28 establishes a similar purpose for work and wealth; that is, to help those in need: "He who has been stealing must steal no longer, but must work, doing something useful with his own hands, that he may have something to share with those in need."

Overall, the Bible discusses money in two primary roles: investing and giving. Examples of both uses abound throughout the Old and New Testaments, including instructions on how to succeed in both areas—what to do, what not to do, and the proper attitude to have toward money.

INVESTING

In the parable of the talents in Matthew 25:14-30, we learn about the importance of putting money to good use. In the parable, three servants are entrusted with unequal portions of their master's wealth. Two of them work to increase the amount they were given, whereas the third servant simply hides his master's money. The first two, who increase their master's wealth, are rewarded with praise from their master and are entrusted with greater amounts of money. The third man returns the money to his master without investing it. He is berated for his laziness and cast out.

The application of this parable is that Christ is the Master who owns everything, and we are his servants.

We were spiritually born into his house, bought by his blood, and employed to do his work here on earth.

We can learn three important lessons from this story. First, as Christians we are entrusted with our Master's goods, which encompass everything. He owns it all, and we are his stewards. All that we have comes from him, in and of ourselves, we lack true worth. In the story, the master is "like a man going on a journey" who entrusted his property to his servants. In Ephesians 4:8, Paul explains that when Jesus Christ ascended into heaven, he entrusted many things to his people. In writing to Timothy, Paul tells his young protégé to "guard the good deposit that was entrusted to you—guard it with the help of the Holy Spirit who lives in us" (2 Timothy 1:14).

Jesus left us what we need to prosper here on earth, but it should be noted that he did not apportion things equally. To one servant, he left five times as much as another. But in the end, they were not judged according to how much they started with or how they competed with each other. They were judged according to what they had done with what was entrusted to them individually. This is an important truth that must be considered throughout

> Jesus left us what we need to prosper here on earth, but he did not apportion things equally.

this discussion on prosperity—we must not compare ourselves with others. Some individuals obviously possess more natural talent than others. Some are more gifted, more intelligent, and more fortunate. In this fact we must rejoice. If we will submit ourselves to God's will and allow him to use all that he gave us for his glory, then we will find contentment and happiness. When other people accumulate material gain, we must not become jealous. We must rejoice in their success and pray that their focus will remain on God's will.

Second, the master had expectations of his servants. Regardless of their allotted portion, each servant was expected to invest well, work hard, and reap the rewards. According to the law of reaping and sowing, the servants merely had to follow the instructions of their master, utilizing what had been entrusted to them in order to prosper. It was only the third servant, who gave in to his fear, who did not prosper. It could be argued that because he returned the full sum to his master, he did not actually fail, but the parable makes it very clear that God does not intend for us to simply maintain what he has given us. We are to utilize it "to prepare God's people for works of service, so that the body of Christ may be built up" (Ephesians 4:12).

Third, we will be held accountable for our handling of our Master's wealth. Jesus' return is promised, as is a great reckoning, and we should work to prepare for that day. Are we using our gifts—spiritual and material—to further his Kingdom? Or are we simply enjoying a comfortable life on our Master's dime?

Are we too afraid to step out and invest his wealth in order to expand his influence?

Christ compels us to take what he has entrusted to us and invest it wisely so that others may come into his Kingdom. Whether we have been given wisdom, knowledge, talents (aptitudes, skills, and abilities), or money, we must sow it in good soil—not keep it or hide it; that is, we must put it to good use.

Notice that the two wise servants looked for a return on their investment. They did not squander it or allow it to sit idle. They sowed it in good soil and expected a return. They put it to work according to God's principles and had faith that more would return. When we have the faith to trust God that his Word is true and that his laws are sound, we do not operate in fear or with selfish motives.

Our wealth is not our own—it is the Lord's. He has

> The two wise servants looked for a return on their investment. They did not squander it or allow it to sit idle. They sowed it in good soil and expected a return.

entrusted it to us, and we must use it for his glory, not our own. We must invest the Lord's money and other resources wisely, according to his principles in the Bible and according to his revelation through the Holy Spirit, in order to increase his Kingdom. For we are not our own but God's alone; and as his Kingdom prospers, we prosper in it.

GIVING

In Matthew 25, immediately following the parable about investing, Jesus teaches another lesson—this one on giving. Many people do not distinguish between the parable of the talents and the story about separating the sheep and the goats, but there are many differences:

> *When the Son of Man comes in his glory, and all the angels with him, he will sit on his throne in heavenly glory. All the nations will be gathered before him, and he will separate the people one from another as a shepherd separates the sheep from the goats. He will put the sheep on his right and the goats on his left.*
>
> *Then the King will say to those on his right, "Come, you who are blessed by my Father; take your inheritance, the kingdom prepared for you since the creation of the world. For I was hungry and you*

*gave me something to eat, I was thirsty and you
gave me something to drink, I was a stranger and
you invited me in, I needed clothes and you clothed
me, I was sick and you looked after me, I was in
prison and you came to visit me."*

*Then the righteous will answer him, "Lord, when
did we see you hungry and feed you, or thirsty and
give you something to drink? When did we see you
a stranger and invite you in, or needing clothes and
clothe you? When did we see you sick or in prison
and go to visit you?"*

*The King will reply, "I tell you the truth, whatever
you did for one of the least of these brothers of mine,
you did for me."*

*Then he will say to those on his left, "Depart
from me, you who are cursed, into the eternal fire
prepared for the devil and his angels. For I was
hungry and you gave me nothing to eat, I was
thirsty and you gave me nothing to drink, I was
a stranger and you did not invite me in, I needed
clothes and you did not clothe me, I was sick and
in prison and you did not look after me."*

*They also will answer, "Lord, when did we see
you hungry or thirsty or a stranger or needing
clothes or sick or in prison, and did not help you?"*

He will reply, "I tell you the truth, whatever you

did not do for one of the least of these, you did not do for me."

Then they will go away to eternal punishment, but the righteous to eternal life. (vv. 31-46)

Share—with Gladness in Your Heart

In this great passage in Matthew 25, Jesus clearly tells us that we absolutely must take care of those in need. Those who lack food, water, covering, freedom, and health deserve our help *with no expectation of return.* When our ministry helps to feed the hungry children of Africa, we do not expect our efforts to develop into a profitable business venture. Never has our chief financial officer said, "If we help feed *x* number of children for *x* number of years, we should start seeing a return on our investment in ten years." We expect no monetary return on our charity.

If the focus is on the return, then why give charitably? If we have that frame of mind, there is no good reason. As Christians, we give out of obedience to Jesus Christ and out of compassion for those who suffer. Both of those reasons merit our gifts. Jesus said to give to those in need, so we give to those in need. In the process, we share God's love. The Bible says that the world will know that we are Christians by our love. How can we pretend to love someone if we don't meet his or her most basic needs? Even non-Christians can show compassion toward the suffering, so why shouldn't Christ's followers show compassion all the more? If we really love the Lord, we will give cheerfully, and without strings attached, to meet the needs of the world.

Robert Morris, my pastor and friend, gave a great illustration of this principle in his teaching titled "The Blessed Life." Consider this modern-day parable:

Suppose I have to go on an extended journey, and I choose three men for a special responsibility. I say to those three men, "I'm going to send you each $10,000 every month. You may keep $9,000 of the money and spend it as you please. But I want you to give $1,000 each month to my wife for the meeting of her needs."

As promised, I send each of these men $10,000 monthly. After a few months, I call my wife and ask her if she is receiving the support I had arranged. Her reply is, "Well, the first one is sending $1,000, just as you instructed him. The second one is actually sending $2,000 a month. I don't know why, but he is. But the third one sent me $800 the first month, $300 the second month, and nothing the third month."

Now, as her husband who loves her with all my heart, what do you think I'm going to do? I am the one providing the money to these men. I've told them they can keep $9,000 for themselves. All I wanted them to do was give a mere 10 percent so there could be food in my house [see Malachi 3:10].

Well, with the first man, who was being faithful to follow my instructions, I am going to continue sending him that $10,000. But for the third man—the one who wasn't satisfied with the 90 percent I graciously gave him—I am going to quit sending him $10,000 a month and send it to the generous man, instead. Why? Because I can trust the second man. He has demonstrated that he cares about what I care about. He is a good steward.

With our finances, we can choose to follow God's instructions to care for the things he cares about, or we can choose to be concerned only with ourselves. But when we learn to give generously—regardless of a set "law" about tithing—we truly earn God's trust. He honors a cheerful giver and a wise and faithful steward. Our hearts must be so in tune with God's that we become what he wants us to become in every way—including in our use of finances.

CARING FOR OUR FAMILIES AND OTHERS

We are to take care of our families. Paul makes this very clear in his first letter to Timothy: "If anyone does not provide for his relatives, and especially for his immediate family, he has denied the faith and is worse than an unbeliever" (5:8).

In another letter, this one to the church in Corinth, Paul makes the statement that "children should not have to save up for their parents, but parents for their children" (2 Corinthians 12:14). This implies a level of parental responsibility that is proper in the eyes of the Lord. Certainly we must take care of our family's needs. However, this does not make a case for a lifestyle of excess. Taking care of our families means providing food, clothing, shelter, and other basic necessities. It does not mean wasting money on frivolous items in order to pacify our selfish desires to accumulate possessions or impress others with our wealth.

It is honorable and right to care for our families. Often this will require extra work or sacrifice on our part—whether it's putting in overtime at work, cutting back on personal expenses, paying child support on time, or taking in an elderly parent. But clearly we bear the responsibility to take care of our relatives in legitimate need.

This principle can also be applied spiritually in the sense that we should also care for those in need within the body of Christ. Our heavenly Father blesses those who help take care of his children. In Isaiah 58, the people of God ask the Lord why they have missed out on his blessings:

"Why have we fasted," they say,
    "and you have not seen it?
Why have we humbled ourselves,
    and you have not noticed?" (v. 3)

Here, the people claim that they have made sacrifices for God. They believe that they have taken the proper religious steps to satisfy God, yet they feel neglected by their Creator. The Lord responds to their claims with a rebuke:

"On the day of your fasting, you do as you please
    and exploit all your workers.
Your fasting ends in quarreling and strife,
    and in striking each other with wicked fists.
You cannot fast as you do today
    and expect your voice to be heard on high.
Is this the kind of fast I have chosen,
    only a day for a man to humble himself?
Is it only for bowing one's head like a reed
    and for lying on sackcloth and ashes?
Is that what you call a fast,
    a day acceptable to the Lord?" (vv. 3-5)

For all their religious activities, their lives were a mess! They fought among themselves, treated their subordinates poorly, and lived their lives however they wished. (Certainly, there are parallels between the people of Israel and today's church.) To help the people understand the true nature of his desired "sacrifice," the Lord spelled it out clearly for them:

> *"Is not this the kind of fasting I have chosen:*
> *to loose the chains of injustice*
>   *and untie the cords of the yoke,*
> *to set the oppressed free*
>   *and break every yoke?*
> *Is it not to share your food with the hungry*
>   *and to provide the poor wanderer with shelter—*
> *when you see the naked, to clothe him,*
>   *and not to turn away from your own flesh and*
>   *blood?"* (vv. 6-7)

The offering that the Lord wanted from his people in Old Testament times and still wants from his church today is that we would live in freedom and share our abundance with the hungry, the homeless poor, and the naked. This is not only literal but spiritual as well. Those who are hungry for spiritual truth must hear it from us. Those who have strayed from home must be loved back into the shelter of the Almighty. And we must, in love, cover the nakedness of our Christian brothers and sisters.

Often, believers are afraid to acknowledge their failures to other Christians for fear of being exposed, ridiculed, or ostracized. Many Christians do not live with the confidence that the love of God covers them and leads them away from defeat and darkness. They are afraid of what other Christians will say about them if they open up in honesty. I have seen many church leaders who have failed who live in fear of what other church leaders would say about them or do to them if they dared to confess their sins, either privately or openly.

As believers who are part of the family of God, we must learn to cover the nakedness of those who fail by helping them find restoration and forgiveness through repentance. Rather than exposing the failures of our fallen brothers and sisters in Christ, we cover them with the love of our heavenly Father, who welcomes returning prodigals.

> *"Then your light will break forth like the dawn,*
>   *and your healing will quickly appear;*
> *then your righteousness will go before you,*
>   *and the glory of the Lord will be your rear*
>   *guard.*
> *Then you will call, and the Lord will answer;*
>   *you will cry for help, and he will say: Here*
>   *am I."* (vv. 8-9)

God says that our light will break out like the dawn
and our own recovery will speedily spring forth. Our
righteousness, which is actually his righteousness
poured out through us, will lead us, and the glory of
God will be our rear-guard protection. Then we will
call on God, and he will answer. We will experience
his presence.

If we give to the hungry and seek to satisfy the desire
of the afflicted, then our light will arise in the midst of
the darkness that prevails in the lives of so many. Our
own gloom—the challenges of life—will become like
midday brightness, and God will continually guide us.
He will satisfy our desires even in the scorched and difficult places; even in economically challenging times,
God will satisfy our desires. But remember, because we
are now abiding in him, he is giving us the desires of
our hearts, and our hearts' desires have changed
because God himself has become our delight.

As we accomplish the Lord's purpose on earth, we
become like a watered garden—fruitful. We become a
river of life, and God says the spring of water will not
fail. We will rebuild the important foundations in our
lives and the lives of those we touch. We will repair the
breach in the wall of truth and restore the pleasant
places and streets where people live. As King David
says in Psalm 23, the Lord will lead us into green

pastures (supplying our needs) and lead us to lie down by still waters (calming us by his abiding presence).

CARING FOR THE POOR

If anyone has material possessions and sees his brother in need but has no pity on him, how can the love of God be in him? (1 JOHN 3:17)

Most monetary references in the Scriptures deal with giving to the poor and the needy. It could be argued that the primary purpose for money in the lives of Christians is to enable us to meet the practical needs of others. Indeed, if our purpose in life is to share the gospel of Jesus Christ so that others may know him, it stands to reason that Christians should be financially able to provide food, clothing, water, shelter, and other basic needs of life in order to open the door to witnessing.

Consider these examples of the numerous axioms and illustrations about caring for those in need found throughout the Old and New Testaments:

Blessed is he who has regard for the weak;
the Lord delivers him in times of trouble.
The Lord will protect him and preserve his life;

he will bless him in the land
and not surrender him to the desire of his foes.
The Lord will sustain him on his sickbed
and restore him from his bed of illness.
(PSALM 41:1-3)

He who oppresses the poor shows contempt for
their Maker,
but whoever is kind to the needy honors God.
(PROVERBS 14:31)

If a man shuts his ears to the cry of the poor,
he too will cry out and not be answered.
(PROVERBS 21:13)

He who gives to the poor will lack nothing,
but he who closes his eyes to them receives
many curses.   (PROVERBS 28:27)

The righteous care about justice for the poor,
but the wicked have no such concern.
(PROVERBS 29:7)

Speak up and judge fairly; defend the rights of
the poor and needy.   (PROVERBS 31:9)

*Now this was the sin of your sister Sodom: She
and her daughters were arrogant, overfed and
unconcerned; they did not help the poor and needy.*
(EZEKIEL 16:49)

*"What should we do then?" the crowd asked. John
answered, "The man with two tunics should share
with him who has none, and the one who has food
should do the same."* (LUKE 3:10-11)

*But give what is inside [the temple] to the poor, and
everything will be clean for you.* (LUKE 11:41)

Sell your possessions and give to the poor.
(LUKE 12:33)

*Then Jesus said to his host, "When you give a
luncheon or dinner, do not invite your friends, your
brothers or relatives, or your rich neighbors; if you
do, they may invite you back and so you will be
repaid. But when you give a banquet, invite the
poor, the crippled, the lame, the blind, and you
will be blessed. Although they cannot repay you, you
will be repaid at the resurrection of the righteous."*
(LUKE 14:12-14)

Selling their possessions and goods, they gave to anyone as he had need. (ACTS 2:45)

At Caesarea there was a man named Cornelius, a centurion in what was known as the Italian Regiment. He and all his family were devout and God-fearing; he gave generously to those in need and prayed to God regularly. One day at about three in the afternoon he had a vision. He distinctly saw an angel of God, who came to him and said, "Cornelius!" Cornelius stared at him in fear. "What is it, Lord?" he asked. The angel answered, "Your prayers and gifts to the poor have come up as a memorial offering before God." (ACTS 10:1-4)

But just as you excel in everything—in faith, in speech, in knowledge, in complete earnestness and in your love for us—see that you also excel in this grace of giving. I am not commanding you, but I want to test the sincerity of your love by comparing it with the earnestness of others."
(2 CORINTHIANS 8:7-8)

For if the willingness is there, the gift is acceptable according to what one has, not according to what he does not have. (2 CORINTHIANS 8:12)

99

All they asked was that we should continue to remember the poor, the very thing I was eager to do. (GALATIANS 2:10)

This is how we know what love is: Jesus Christ laid down his life for us. And we ought to lay down our lives for our brothers. If anyone has material possessions and sees his brother in need but has no pity on him, how can the love of God be in him? Dear children, let us not love with words or tongue but with actions and in truth. (1 JOHN 3:16-18)

It is interesting to note that when the government seeks to achieve a "redistribution of the wealth" through secular socialism or Marxism, it fails every time. Only when the wealthy are divinely inspired to focus their attention on the needs of others do we see success in helping the poor. God places great value on giving to the poor. It should be equally as urgent with us. Remember, God will bless us when we give to those who may never be able to pay us back. When we help the helpless, God becomes our almighty helper.

LENDING

Beyond meeting others' basic needs, we're also called to another form of charity: lending to those who ask.

We should be open to this, even to the point of lending to our enemies with no expectation of payback.

> *Give to the one who asks you, and do not turn away from the one who wants to borrow from you.*
> (MATTHEW 5:42)

> *If you lend to those from whom you expect repayment, what credit is that to you? Even "sinners" lend to "sinners," expecting to be repaid in full. But love your enemies, do good to them, and lend to them without expecting to get anything back.* (LUKE 6:34-35)

> *Command those who are rich in this present world not to be arrogant nor to put their hope in wealth, which is so uncertain, but to put their hope in God, who richly provides us with everything for our enjoyment. Command them to do good, to be rich in good deeds, and to be generous and willing to share.*
> (1 TIMOTHY 6:17-18)

When lending to people in need, we must do so without expecting them to pay us back. Never lend if the borrower's failure to pay you back would strain your relationship. Share in love, and enjoy blessing those in need. If they do pay it back, consider it another blessing from God.

Although we're to lend with no expectation of return, it doesn't mean we shouldn't allow borrowers to pay us back. Even if we lend money that we could otherwise give, we should understand that it is often important for borrowers to learn to fulfill their financial responsibilities by paying back what they have borrowed. Be a wise teacher for their sake, and graciously allow what is in the borrower's best interest.

TITHING

One cannot be around the church for very long without hearing about tithing, which is the practice of giving to God the first 10 percent of our earnings. In the earliest recorded history, people offered the firstfruits of their harvest and their herds to the Lord (see Genesis 4:3-4). Later, the principle of tithing was encoded in the laws of the nation of Israel (see Numbers 18:25-32; Deuteronomy 14:22-29). The purpose of the tithe was twofold: to place God in the forefront of people's daily lives and to make sure that nobody lacked for food. In this way, both great commandments of Christ are expressed: love God and love your neighbor.

> *A tithe of everything from the land, whether grain from the soil or fruit from the trees, belongs to the Lord; it is holy to the Lord.* (LEVITICUS 27:30)

When you have finished setting aside a tenth of all your produce in the third year, the year of the tithe, you shall give it to the Levite, the alien, the fatherless and the widow, so that they may eat in your towns and be satisfied.

(DEUTERONOMY 26:12)

Honor the Lord with your wealth,
    with the firstfruits of all your crops;
then your barns will be filled to overflowing,
    and your vats will brim over with new wine.
    (PROVERBS 3:9-10)

"Bring the whole tithe into the storehouse, that there may be food in my house. Test me in this," says the Lord Almighty, "and see if I will not throw open the floodgates of heaven and pour out so much blessing that you will not have room enough for it."

(MALACHI 3:10)

Woe to you Pharisees, because you give God a tenth of your mint, rue and all other kinds of garden herbs, but you neglect justice and the love of God. You should have practiced the latter without leaving the former undone.   (LUKE 11:42)

It is important to note in Luke 11:42 that Jesus scorned the religious Pharisees for obeying the letter of the law while failing to adhere to the spirit of the law. Though Christ focuses on their hearts, and finds them lacking, he also acknowledges that they were proper in their practice of tithing.

My pastor, Robert Morris, puts it this way in his book *The Blessed Life:*

> The first belongs to God. We find this principle all through God's Word. We can give God the first of our time. We can give Him the first of our finances. That's really what tithing is—giving our first to God.
>
> It always requires faith to give the first. That's why so few Christians experience the blessings of tithing. It means giving to God before you see if you're going to have enough. In tithing, we say to God, "I recognize You first. I am putting You first in my life, and I trust You to take care of the rest of the things in my life."

Many pastors point out that the "storehouse" to which Malachi refers (in Malachi 3:10) was the local place where people in need went to be fed. In making application of this passage, they often spiritualize the idea of feeding to mean the place where people go to be fed spiritually—namely, the local church. However, even though they understand "feeding" in a spiritual sense, they always interpret literally the 10 percent that we're to give. The standard teaching is that Christians must give 10 percent of their income to the local church.

However, we have a responsibility to consider the place to which we tithe. Are people being fed spiritually and literally? Or are we padding the pockets of a preacher so that he can build unnecessary buildings, fulfill his personal ambitions, or live an exorbitant lifestyle? If a needy member of the church family seeks help from the "storehouse" to which you tithe, will that person's need be met? If not, we should reexamine our tithe.

Obviously, no single church or ministry can meet every need of every person. However, the recipient of our tithes should demonstrate a desire to meet real needs and provide real evidence of doing so. It must be a ministry not only in word but also in deed (see 1 John 3:18).

Truly, God owns everything, and he asks us to participate with him by releasing the tithe for his Kingdom purposes. This is a simple but important starting point in financial responsibility. The principle of giving our firstfruits is scriptural and should be active in our lives, but the tithe must be accomplishing its intended purpose—to expand the Kingdom of God and help to meet the legitimate needs of people. The storehouse is certainly not to be interpreted as a building

The principle of giving our firstfruits is scriptural and should be active in our lives. or an institution. Rather it is God's way of fulfilling his Kingdom purpose and providing for those who face a crisis or shortfall.

An interesting passage of Scripture—one that rarely appears in sermons, much less sermons on prosperity—suggests some interesting ramifications for how we use money:

> *He who oppresses the poor to increase his wealth and he who gives gifts to the rich—both come to poverty.* (PROVERBS 22:16)

Matthew Henry, the respected nineteenth-century Bible scholar, says that this verse refers to people who ignore the needs of the poor while wasting money trying to gain the favor of other rich or powerful people. "Many have been beggared by a foolish generosity," he writes, "but never any by a prudent charity."[9] Truly we have witnessed the financial ruin that many well-intentioned yet foolish people have come to because they have given great sums of money to prosperity peddlers in an attempt to bribe God into action. "You can't out-give God!" many exclaim. And though this is certainly true—indeed we cannot outdo God in any area—we can certainly waste by foolish generosity what God has entrusted to us for proper use. Compulsive, desperate, self-motivated giving is not an offering; it is waste. Many gifts have been wasted or poorly invested through grants to institutions of so-called higher learning that actually attack our faith in God and the free enterprise system that enables our economic prosperity.

QUESTIONS & ANSWERS

How much of my money belongs to God?

Perhaps the most important question related to our finances is how much of it really belongs to God—not just in theory but in reality. Three possibilities exist, which we should examine on both a practical and a spiritual level.

First, we could consider all of the wealth we possess as ours. It was earned by our own hands, entrusted to us by God, and we are to use it as we see fit. After all, in the parable of the talents in Matthew 25, the servant said, "Master, you have entrusted me with five talents. See, I have gained five more" (v. 20). Jesus praised him for his faithful service. The servant did not give one talent to the church, live off of two, and put the other two in the bank—he kept them all and invested them as he saw fit.

Second, we could consider 10 percent of our wealth as a tithe to our local church or ministry. Malachi 3:10 says, "Bring the whole tithe into the storehouse . . . and see if I will not throw open the floodgates of heaven and pour out so much blessing that you will not have room enough for it." So we simply give one-tenth of our income to charity, write it off on our taxes, and spend the rest however we wish—on houses, cars, vacations, and the necessities of life.

Third, we could consider all of our wealth as belonging to the Lord. "The earth is the Lord's, and everything in it" (Psalm 24:1). Therefore, we actually own nothing, even though it may be in our possession. We are stewards of the Master's resources.

We actually own nothing, even though it may be in our possession. We are stewards of the Master's resources.

Our true perspective on this issue affects everything we do. It shapes our spending habits, influences how we spend our leisure time, and determines our charitable giving. Our answer to the question *How much of my money belongs to God?* directly determines how we will answer every other financial question in our lives.

In the first scenario, we would be bound to financial growth, reaping the monetary rewards of our efforts endlessly, because our godliness would be measured by our gain. In the second scenario, we simply need to pay God a commission so that we can enjoy the rest of our wealth as we see fit. In the third scenario, we are accountable for every penny we spend because we are not overseeing our own money but God's. In fact, the parable of the talents points to the fact that the money we have is not ours—it's *entrusted* to us. The lesson is not so much about investment skills as it is about properly using what God has entrusted to us in a way that pleases the Master. Most people do not consciously live in the third scenario. Most of us strive to give our 10 percent to God's Kingdom work and then spend the rest however we please. For some, that simply means paying the bills. For others, it means lavish homes, extravagant cars, expensive hobbies, and exotic vacations. For far too many people, it means poor money management and an accumulation of debt.

Read this next paragraph very carefully. It encapsulates an important truth about true prosperity.

Somewhere there exists a balance between poverty and excess. It is a place where our needs are met, with enough left over to help others. It is a place where we acknowledge that everything belongs to God, who truly owns everything on the earth—a God who is never short of cash and who trusts us to use his wealth to glorify him 100 percent as his Spirit and his Word direct us.

What does it mean to lay up treasures in heaven?

Do not store up for yourselves treasures on earth, where moth and rust destroy, and where thieves break in and steal. But store up for yourselves treasures in heaven, where moth and rust do not destroy, and where thieves do not break in and steal. For where your treasure is, there your heart will be also.

The eye is the lamp of the body. If your eyes are good, your whole body will be full of light. But if your eyes are bad, your whole body will be full of darkness. If then the light within you is darkness, how great is that darkness!

No one can serve two masters. Either he will hate the one and love the other, or he will be devoted to the one and despise the other. You cannot serve both God and Money. (MATTHEW 6:19-24)

Traditional teaching on this passage emphasizes the importance of doing things that focus on eternal results—preaching the gospel, comforting those in distress, praying for others, feeding the hungry, and so on.

These pursuits are in contrast to the ways of the world, where power and wealth capture people's hearts. The passage culminates with these oft-quoted words: "You cannot serve both God and Money," which reflects the first commandment, "You shall have no other gods before me" (Exodus 20:3). If we are to serve God, we must serve him exclusively. There can be no competition. Everything is surrendered to him.

In contrast to the traditional understanding of Matthew 6:19-24, an interesting interpretation has cropped up among some contemporary teachers. It goes something like this: If we will give our money to God (in the form of donations to a prosperity preacher or ministry), it will be deposited into a "heavenly bank account," where it will stay until we need it (for a new car, bigger house, or whatever our hearts desire). Thus, by believing in our own faith, we can withdraw this money whenever we wish.

"By giving," one teacher writes, "heaven declares certain portions as mine. No force on earth then is able to keep it from coming to me when I call for it!"[10] But is God merely setting up a great credit union in the sky for us, or is he pointing us beyond worldly riches to a greater glory? First Corinthians 9:25 refers to an eternal crown rewarded to those who serve others for the sake of the gospel. Truly, the treasure we lay up in heaven lies in the souls reached for Christ through our obedience here on earth and in the things accomplished through lives yielded to the Holy Spirit.

I heard a good story that illustrates the biblical principle of laying up treasures in heaven. Brian, a man who works for our ministry, Life Outreach International, and his wife, Laurie, have lived a modest lifestyle. They both worked to make ends meet and to pay off college loans. One day Brian received a call from the pastor of a small church. Their building desperately needed painting and someone had mentioned that Brian did some painting on the side. After meeting with the pastor and assessing the size of the job, Brian went home to write up a quote. Ordinarily, a project of that size would earn him about four thousand dollars—much-needed cash that could be used to pay some bills and reduce his family's debt. He considered offering the pastor a generous discount, but he could not shake the notion that God had something else in mind. After wrestling with it for a couple of days, he decided to take what was on his heart to his wife.

"Laurie, you know that church I'm writing up a quote for?" he asked.

"You're supposed to do it for free, aren't you?" she replied.

Brian was astounded. "That's exactly what I've been thinking," he said.

He told the pastor that he believed he was to donate his time and effort if the church would purchase the supplies. The pastor accepted the offer, and Brian went to work. Several days later he finished the job and the church members enjoyed an updated, beautified building.

A week later the pastor came to visit Brian. "We appreciate your work and your attitude," he said. "So we took up an offering on Sunday to thank you." The pastor pulled out a check and handed it to Brian. It was for five thousand dollars—20 percent more than Brian would have typically earned on a similar job. Although he was very thankful and accepted the check, he couldn't shake the feeling that the money was just not his. He had given his services expecting nothing in return, yet the church had graciously blessed him.

When he arrived home that evening, he found his wife crying. "What's wrong?" he asked.

Laurie, who taught at an elementary school, told Brian that there were two young siblings there who were extremely poor. They were restless and hard to teach. Their few clothes were ragged, and they ate their lunches as if they hadn't eaten anything at home. Their single mother worked hard to take care of them, and she truly loved them. Yet, she had no car, so she was stuck in a low-paying job near their low-rent apartment. Laurie's heart was broken for them, and she wished she could do something to help.

Brian pulled out the check.

"The church gave this to me for my work," he said. "But if you want to give it to this poor family, I think we should." Laurie agreed, but she wanted to give the gift anonymously. The next day she obtained a cashier's check and gave it to the mother. "Someone heard your story and wanted to bless you," she told her, "but they want to remain anonymous." The mother broke down in tears, grateful for the unexpected gift.

That weekend the single mother bought a used car. Within two weeks she got a new job—one that paid twice as much as her old one and included family health care and other wonderful benefits. Within a month, the two children had new clothes. By the end of the year, the children were A-level students, progressing in knowledge and discipline.

Brian and Laurie received no multiplied financial gift in the ensuing weeks. They gave in obedience, not in greed. But they shared the joy of seeing a whole family changed forever.

Just before publication of this book, Brian and Laurie had their own family changed forever when God opened the way for them to adopt a baby boy, fulfilling a lifelong desire of theirs to be parents. As Brian and Laurie continue to trust God for their needs, focusing on laying up treasures in heaven, God continues to bless their faithfulness to him by exceeding their expectations.

CHAPTER 5

RELEASING THE RIVER

A generous person quickly discovers that each new day
provides new opportunities to impact the lives of others.
Every day we can find countless ways—great and
small—to make someone's life better.

S. TRUETT CATHY

GOD HAS blessed Betty and me tremendously. We've never personally been in the bondage of debt or gone through the financial struggles that many people have experienced. One reason is that we have never sought "stuff." Our philosophy has always been: "Can't afford it? Don't buy it." We have always lived well below our means. From the time we married, we paid by cash or check for everything, or if we used a bank card, it was paid in full each month. We actually budgeted to live on 50 percent to 75 percent of our monthly income and still do to this day.

Our first home was a ten-foot-by-fifty-foot trailer. We had a king-size bed—and let me tell you, that bed filled our room. A few years later we bought a small house. As I recall, our monthly payments were just over $100. A short time later, when our ministry had a need, Betty and I decided to sell our house. We gave the entire $12,000 in equity to the ministry. Although it represented a lot of money to us, we never expected to get a thirty-, sixty-, or hundredfold return. In fact, Betty and I have never given with a focus on getting a return, because we live knowing that God has focused his love on us and all his children.

Shortly after we sold our home, I shared Christ with a local woman and her family. They lived in a small, rural home, with meager means. I had taken her troubled teenage nephew with me to a crusade, and it had changed his life. My visit was a wonderful time of ministry, but I didn't expect to see the woman again. However, within a few months, she walked in the door of our ministry with a check for $109,000, part of the proceeds she had received from selling her small house, which happened to be located on the property where the Dallas–Fort Worth International Airport would soon be built. She had received almost $2 million for her modest home.

"I want to help you start your television ministry,"

she said. She also told us she had heard Betty and me talk about desiring to take care of the pastor and his wife who had given me a home for the first five years of my childhood, as well as for a couple of my high school years. "I want you to take care of them," she said, "and I am buying you a house so you can do that." She paid cash for a home that Betty and I shared with my foster parents for a number of years.

We later sold that house and gave the money to the ministry, trusting God to take care of us. Once again he showed us favor by giving us what proved to be supernatural insight and wisdom. About thirty years ago, he led us to the piece of property where we built our next home and still live today. It was outside of town, overlooking a flood plain, and the land wasn't considered valuable. However, it was perfect for our family because it had space for a nice yard where our children could play, and it gave us some privacy. Twenty-five years later, our property sits in one of the most sought-after areas in the Dallas–Fort Worth metroplex, with some land values multiplying more than 100 times! Only God could have known about the increase that was in store. Betty and I did not choose the area for its investment potential but

Only God could have known about the increase that was in store.

rather to invest in our family's future—and God blessed us beyond our wildest imagination. A few years ago we were able to refinance our house and use the appreciated value to buy a half interest in a small wildlife ranch, where we often rest, meditate, and do some writing.

My intention is not to single out my family's experience. I imagine that many others could add examples of phenomenal blessing to the list. My point is that far too many people are not hearing what God wants them to hear—they are hearing what Western culture and some out-of-balance ministers are teaching. I am convinced that our hearts must change until "giving to get" is no longer the major motivating factor in our decisions. It is only when we have presented ourselves to God as living sacrifices and have committed fully to do his will that he will reveal his perfect will to us.

God doesn't want us to play the money game. The Christian life is not a lottery or spiritual bingo. *Giving is the essence of life and is its own reward.* Jesus wants us to understand this principle. If we release what he has freely given to us, I believe with all my heart that he will supply the increase—not so we can build bigger barns but so we can know what it means to live life abundantly. Those who focus on earthly treasures and on receiving a blessing may get a lot of stuff, but they will not experience fullness of life or fullness of joy. In the end, they will rot in their riches. Possessions do not produce a meaningful life and lasting joy.

Those who focus on earthly treasures and on receiving a blessing may get a lot of stuff, but they will not experience fullness of life or fullness of joy.

Imagine how much the Father in heaven wants to bless a child who can be trusted to release his resources—which may include money—for Kingdom purposes. But those who take in God's blessings but never release them become like the Dead Sea—saturated and unable to sustain life. If we become a stopping point, hindering the release of God's resources, we become a dead end. God intends for blessings to flow *through* us, like a river, not just *to* us, like the Dead Sea.

The apostle Paul touches on the river principle in 2 Corinthians 8:15, where he writes, "He who gathered much did not have too much, and he who gathered little did not have too little." The nature of a river is that *whatever it receives, it releases*. That's what makes it a river. No matter how much water flows through, it never seems to have more—and no matter how much it releases, it never has less, because everything flows through it and is used to benefit others. Even when it appears ready to overflow its banks, just keep watching, because it is still continuously releasing everything it has received for the purpose of giving life.

If we decide to live our lives like a river—to release everything that God entrusts to us for his eternal purposes—the results will be amazing. What does a river do when it courses through the earth? Everywhere it flows, life springs up.

Jesus said, "Whoever believes in me . . . streams of living water will flow from within him" (John 7:38). The next verse reveals that he was referring to the Holy Spirit, who was not yet released because Christ had not yet been glorified. But the Spirit would soon be freely flowing everywhere, bringing abundance of life. This is the life that God wants to flow through you and me— just as it did through the apostles and the early church (see Acts 2:44-47).

BLESS AND YOU WILL BE BLESSED

Another key aspect of the river principle is that the headwater region is the first recipient of everything that is released downstream. In other words, just as the river blesses every place it flows, so, too, the headwaters spring forth with abundant life. So even though the nature of a river is to release its water, the river itself is the first to receive. Take note of the huge trees that grow along the banks of creeks and rivers, providing shade and shelter.

If we bless, we will be blessed. When we focus on releasing all the resources that God entrusts to us—not storing up bigger things, hanging on, hoarding them up, trying to protect them, trying to guard them, and living in absolute misery—we will experience the joy of abundant living even as we release the flow of abundant life to others. Only then will we actually experience the reality of "God giving us all things richly to enjoy."

Second Corinthians 8:9 says, "For you know the grace of our Lord Jesus Christ, that though he was rich, yet for your sakes he became poor, so that you through his poverty might become rich." If you take this passage to heart, God promises you will receive much more than material gain. Those who know Christ are rich beyond measure—rich in salvation, forgiveness, joy, peace, glory, and honor. That, my friend, is true prosperity. Once you've received these blessings from above, I encourage you to share them with others so that they, too, can be blessed and know what it means to truly prosper.

Psalm 37:3-4 says, "Trust in the Lord and do good; dwell in the land and enjoy safe pasture. Delight yourself in the Lord and he will give you the desires of your heart." When we truly delight in the Lord, our hearts' desires will conform to the heart of God. When we place our complete trust in the Lord, including our finances, we can live in comfort and security. When our delight is not in our material possessions or ourselves but in the Lord himself, then we will discover that God continually gives good gifts to his children. Our desires will be in line with his desires.

BE A FARMER, NOT A MINER

The concept of sowing and reaping is an important aspect of giving. Unfortunately, it has become so distorted in recent years that many people have missed out on the intended meaning. Look at what the apostle Paul says about the law of the harvest—and notice how the emphasis is on *giving,* not on *receiving:*

> Remember this: Whoever sows sparingly will also reap sparingly, and whoever sows generously will also reap generously. Each man should give what he has decided in his heart to give, not reluctantly or under compulsion, for God loves a cheerful giver. And God is able to make all grace abound to you, so that in all things at all times, having all that you need, you will abound in every good work. As it is written: "He has scattered abroad his gifts to the poor; his righteousness endures forever."

Now he who supplies seed to the sower and bread for food will also supply and increase your store of seed and will enlarge the harvest of your righteousness. You will be made rich in every way so that you can be generous on every occasion, and through us your generosity will result in thanksgiving to God.
(2 CORINTHIANS 9:6-11)

Have you ever observed a farmer? He prepares the ground, plants the seeds, tends the crop, prays for sun and rain—*and no matter what happens, he will plant again.* The sun may dry up his harvest, the floods may carry it away, or animals may plunder it, but regardless of the outcome, the farmer sows with the hope of reaping a bountiful harvest sometime in the future. Why? Because he is a farmer—he continually invests in the ground, improving it and trusting God for the increase.

Contrast the approach of the farmer with that of a miner. The miner plunders the earth, digging for riches, and when the earth is depleted, he abandons the mine to look elsewhere for more resources. Why? Because he is a miner—he works the land for profit, sifting through it, taking what he can, and moving on to other potential opportunities. There is no increase in the value of the property, only depletion of the resources.

A woman came to me distraught after hearing me share this example. Her father was a coal miner, and she thought I was implying that he was not a good man. Somehow the spiritual truth I was trying to impart missed the mark with her. I understand her point, and it wasn't my intention to disparage the mining industry. But the truth remains the same: When a miner has depleted the resources or treasures within the mine, the land is devalued and the miner moves on. As a result of this reality, mining companies are now encouraged, and often required, to improve the environment around their mines.

In the natural realm, it makes sense to move from one productive mine to the next. But spiritually speaking, we are to have the commitment and characteristics of a farmer (even if our jobs are in the mining industry). In our spiritual lives, we can sow seeds in love, wait for rain and sunshine, pray for protection from destructive forces, and trust the Lord to provide the promised harvest. Or we can go from church to church, from doctrine to doctrine, from ministry to ministry, and dig for gold, even in the realm of faith.

Another important lesson we can learn from the farmer is that not all farmland and effort yield the same harvest. One of the huge deceptions common in personal prosperity teaching is the notion that *every-*

body is going to have a big house, big car, or big income, and that these material possessions are the measure of a person's spiritual depth. This "sameness" mentality is simply not biblical. No two farmers get exactly the same amount of rain and exactly the same yield in their crops. In fact, godly farmers may not have a harvest as abundant as their ungodly neighbors. Farmers all know that if they are committed and faithful, they will see the return—the harvest—in due season. But there is no way to be guaranteed a thirty-, sixty-, or hundredfold return in a given time frame. All of this is left in the hands of our loving Father in heaven.

> One of the huge deceptions common in personal prosperity teaching is the notion that *everybody* is going to have a big house, big car, or big income.

Matthew 5:45 tells us, "He causes his sun to rise on the evil and the good, and sends rain on the righteous and the unrighteous." The man with the most money is not necessarily the most righteous. Indeed, the poorest of the poor may be the holiest of all. If some of the Old Testament prophets "went about in sheepskins and goatskins, destitute, persecuted and mistreated" and "wandered in deserts and mountains, and in caves and holes in the ground"

(Hebrews 11:37-38), surely we cannot conclude that monetary wealth equals wisdom and earthly riches equal righteousness.

Jesus said, "Foxes have holes and birds of the air have nests, but the Son of Man has no place to lay his head" (Luke 9:58). Everyone—even the most righteous individual—will be tested. We may seem to have problems, challenges, and pressures that others don't battle. The apostle Paul, the writer of much of the New Testament and an awesome example of a man committed to the righteousness of Christ, wrote, "I know what it is to be in need, and I know what it is to have plenty" (Philippians 4:12). He made it clear that because true prosperity was a reality, he was content in whatever circumstances he found himself. Through life's challenges, the Lord often gives us opportunities to share a powerful testimony that will minister to others.

Where is your heart? If your primary focus is on the expected return, you are acting like a miner. God wants us to be farmers for his Kingdom. If we are faithful, Scripture says "in due season" we will reap a harvest. "Let us not become weary in doing good, for at the proper time we will reap a harvest if we do not give up" (Galatians 6:9).

QUESTIONS & ANSWERS

Can we always expect a thirty-, sixty-, or hundredfold return on the money we give?

The answer, in a word, is no. Of course, God is not limited. He can make two loaves of bread feed thousands of people, he can put money in the mouth of a fish, and he can make you the winner of a million-dollar prize. But to categorically say that if you give $10 to a ministry God will be obligated to give you $300, $600, or $1000, is nothing short of deception.

Certainly, "the earth is the Lord's, and everything in it" (Psalm 24:1), but the whole concept of giving comes from Christ's sacrificial offering of himself with nothing expected in return. In fact, the oft-quoted verse that says, "Give, and it will be given to you. A good measure, pressed down, shaken together and running over, will be poured into your lap" (Luke 6:38), refers to the way we treat our enemies, not to the way we give to a ministry or church. In fact, Luke 6:35 says, "Love your enemies, do good to them, and lend to them without expecting to get anything back." Lend to others—to your enemies, no less—and expect nothing in return! Christ gave himself up for us, he died for us, "when we were God's enemies" (Romans 5:10), with no guarantee that we would ever give ourselves back to him. In the same way, we are instructed to give to those in need with no thought of getting something back. We give to give; we do not give to get.

We are instructed to give to those in need with no thought of getting something back. We give to give; we do not give to get.

The source for the "hundred-fold return" philosophy that has caused so much confusion can be found in several places in the Bible. In Matthew 13:8, in the parable of the sower of seeds, it says, "Still other seed fell on good soil, where it produced a crop—a hundred, sixty or thirty times what was sown."* In this context, it is clearly talking about the gospel of Jesus Christ. The seed is the Word of God, and the soil represents the hearts of humanity. The crop is the salvation of souls. The message is that the truth of God's Word can enter into open minds (good soil), change lives (produce a crop), and flourish in the world (thirty-, sixty-, or hundredfold).

Jesus again refers to the multiplication effect in Matthew 19:29, when he says, "Everyone who has left houses or brothers or sisters or father or mother or children or fields for my sake will receive a hundred times

---

*A parallel passage is found in Mark 4:1-8.

as much and will inherit eternal life." This verse would seem to indicate a physical, materialistic repayment for following Christ. On some level, it does make sense that God, being a good God, would reward those who leave their houses for his sake by repaying them with bigger, better houses. And certainly there are examples in the Bible of people who sacrificed things for the sake of the Kingdom and received material blessings for their faithfulness. But is it scriptural to assert, as one prosperity preacher has, "I want my hundred houses!"?

When we take this line of thinking to its end, we quickly see the problems with it. If I leave my house in order to become a traveling evangelist and expect a hundred houses later in life, should I expect to someday have two hundred parents if I leave my mother and father in order to preach? And if I leave my three children and eleven grandchildren to work in Africa, distributing food to the needy and sharing the gospel, should I expect to have three hundred children and eleven hundred grandchildren when I get home? God forbid!

So how does this verse make sense? As any missionary can tell you, when they leave their families to go work overseas, they gain a huge extended family in Christ. They have brothers and sisters in Christ who work alongside them. They have children in Christ who look up to them. They have parents in Christ—older mentors who take care of them. And they have houses open to them anytime they need a place to rest—hundreds of them. You see, when we leave our comfort zone to serve others, we are rewarded with relationships that would have never developed had we stayed home. Jesus promises us a reward that far exceeds bricks and boards. He promises to love us through the people we touch with his love.

> When we leave our comfort zone to serve others, we are rewarded with relationships that would have never developed had we stayed home. Jesus promises to love us through the people we touch with his love.

If we question or challenge the so-called prosperity gospel, must we embrace poverty?

When we seek to correct the extremes of the so-called prosperity gospel, we are not embracing poverty. In fact, we must staunchly resist a poverty mentality and work to rescue those living under its curse. At the same time, we should realize that there may be times in the lives of Christians when they do live "hand to mouth," as so many missionaries do worldwide. In reality, it takes much more faith to trust God day to day than it does to trust a fat bank account, yet wealth and a strong economy can plummet as rapidly as the value of some Internet stocks. We must never trust uncertain riches for our security. We must trust in God alone.

Scripturally, there are two levels of poverty. The first kind, sometimes called "extreme poverty" or "absolute poverty" (*ptochoi* in New Testament Greek), refers to someone who has been reduced to a state of abject pauperism, unable to secure the basics of food, water, shelter, and clothing. It is this poverty that drove Lazarus to beg for crumbs at the rich man's gate in Luke 16. This word *ptochoi* is also used to describe the contract between heaven and the state that Jesus Christ entered into on our behalf when he came to earth: "You know the grace of our Lord Jesus Christ, that though he was rich, yet for your sakes he became poor, so that you through his poverty might become rich" (2 Corinthians 8:9).

In our day there is very little abject poverty in the industrialized West. But in widespread areas of Africa, portions of Asia, and pockets across the world, there are people who literally do not know where their next meal will come from. They have no grocery stores, no soup kitchens, and no local charities. The causes of this poverty range from oppressive governments, as in North Korea; to wars, as in the Congo and the Sudan;

to natural disasters, such as famine or flood. Although many Christians live with the devastating results of the sins of others—such as warfare or oppression—there is no reason that any follower of Christ should ever live in a condition of abject poverty. Christians who do not live in such poverty bear a responsibility to help people who do by first giving them food, water, clothing, and shelter, and then by telling them the good news of Jesus Christ—that he died for our sins and that they do not have to live under the curse of poverty any longer. Even those who live in the poorest nations on earth can prosper spiritually and experience a richness of life that comes only through a relationship with Jesus Christ. Morever, God, in his Word, promises to supply all their needs. We must recognize and receive what is being offered through Christ—the forgiveness of sin and the power to overcome poverty.

The other term for poverty in Greek is *penes,* often translated as "poor." It connotes "one who works for his daily bread." Such is the condition of the widow who cheerfully gave her two small copper coins and reaped the praises of Jesus for her faithfulness (see Mark 12:41-44). In our society, this condition is deemed "socially poor." It refers to those people who cannot afford the common level of health care, cannot routinely vacation, and who depend upon each paycheck to purchase the necessities. Again, Scripture requires us to give to the poor, but it generally refers to those whose poverty is a byproduct of human nature and an imperfect world ("the poor you will have always"), rather than those who are cursed.

Rejecting the extremism of some preachers' prosperity gospel is not the same as rejecting prosperity itself. God does bless some people with the wisdom to create wealth and with circumstances that afford great opportunity, but he does so on his own terms, not according to our demands, incantations, or schemes. One teacher suggests that in order to obtain our pre-ordained wealth, we must "get violent in God." But violent men will never force the hand of God. His will and ways are far above our lowly, materialistic desires. It is true that we must resist evil influences with the full force of our faith, but this also means standing against the potential evil of greed and selfishness.

> God blesses some people with the wisdom to create wealth and with circumstances that afford great opportunity, but he does so on his own terms.

With all my heart I believe that God is looking for people who are committed to his purpose and are living to fulfill his will by blessing others. I believe that God is anxious to pour out the blessings he promises in so many passages of Scripture, including the wondrous Psalm 112:

> *Blessed is the man who fears the Lord,*
> *who finds great delight in his commands.*
>
> *His children will be mighty in the land;*
> *the generation of the upright will be blessed.*
> *Wealth and riches are in his house,*
> *and his righteousness endures forever.*
> *Even in darkness light dawns for the upright,*
> *for the gracious and compassionate and*
> *righteous man.*
> *Good will come to him who is generous and lends*
> *freely,*
> *who conducts his affairs with justice.*
> *Surely he will never be shaken;*
> *a righteous man will be remembered forever.*
> *He will have no fear of bad news;*
> *his heart is steadfast, trusting in the Lord.*
> *His heart is secure, he will have no fear;*
> *in the end he will look in triumph on his foes.*
> *He has scattered abroad his gifts to the poor,*
> *his righteousness endures forever;*
> *his horn will be lifted high in honor.*

The wicked man will see and be vexed,
  he will gnash his teeth and waste away;
  the longings of the wicked will come to nothing.

CHAPTER 6

OBSTACLES TO TRUE PROSPERITY

IN AUGUST 2003, millions of people in the northeast United States and southeast Canada experienced a prolonged blackout. With no warning, they lost power—in some places for days. Too often we can lose our spiritual "power connection" as well. Somewhere, something has broken down. The power that should be ours is gone, and we are left in the dark, trying to guess what went wrong. Likewise, many things can short-circuit our path to true prosperity. If we don't correct these problems, we are doomed to grope in the dark. Although the promise of light and energy is there, we will miss it unless our connection to God's power and wisdom is restored.

Consider a regular television set with an aerial antenna. In a large city, we can receive several channels just by plugging the TV in and tuning to the right station. For purposes of our discussion, let's say that channel 7 is the "true prosperity" channel. It provides twenty-four-hour information on how to be truly prosperous. Let's also say that channel 2 is the "entertainment" channel and channel 4 is the "selfish gain" network. If we are tuned to either of these other channels, we still have the ability to prosper simply by switching to channel 7 and learning the truth, but if we are tuned to the wrong station, we'll get the wrong message. God is broadcasting truth on channel 7, but too many people are absorbed with entertainment or selfish gain. We must remove the obstacles presented by the other channels and "tune in" to the truth of God if we want to learn how to prosper. His truth is clearly revealed in his Word and is totally trustworthy.

> Scripture reveals that God is broadcasting wisdom, truth, and understanding that can be heard by spiritually sensitive ears—those that are tuned in to the heart of God.

The first chapter of Proverbs and many similar passages of Scripture reveal that God is broadcasting wisdom, truth, and understanding that can be heard by spiritually sensitive ears—those that are tuned in to the heart of God. Let's consider some of the "channels" that often distract people from the truth.

GREED

For of this you can be sure: No immoral, impure or greedy person—such a man is an idolater—has any inheritance in the kingdom of Christ and of God.
(EPHESIANS 5:5)

The fastest way to undermine true prosperity is to fall into the trap of greed. Greed is an excessive or insatiable desire for selfish gain. Although it is not exclusively a financial term, it is usually associated with money. But it can also apply to food, sex, sports, hobbies, or anything else that cannot be satisfied. When enough is never enough, greed has taken over.

Do not misinterpret the desire to achieve, succeed, or make gains in life (including financial gains) as greed. Focused ambition is not the problem. Greed is the perversion of potentially good and meaningful attempts to be productive. All faithful farmers live in faith, trusting God for the produce and increase according to his will. But working hard for a bountiful harvest does not necessarily indicate greed.

In the Bible, greed is commonly associated with such things as immorality, thievery, and wickedness. Yet in our society, and even in the church, greed is not taken as seriously as these other sins. But God sees our hearts and knows when a discontented, lustful spirit takes control and begins to affect our thoughts and actions. Greed must be vanquished or else clear insight and direction will be impossible and true prosperity, regardless of our financial status, will forever remain out of reach.

ENVY

A heart at peace gives life to the body, but envy rots the bones. (PROVERBS 14:30)

Envy can be defined as a "painful or resentful awareness of an advantage enjoyed by another joined with a desire to possess the same advantage."[11] When our minds dwell on what others have and we don't (whether materialistic or otherwise), to the point that it becomes painful for us not to have the same possessions, envy sets in and sucks the life out of us. But whatever it is that we envy is not worth the loss of peace and joy.

In their respective Gospels, Matthew and Mark both point out that the chief priests handed Jesus over to

Pilate to be crucified because of their envy (see Matthew 27:18; Mark 15:10). As religious leaders, they wanted Christ's authority, power, and position. But even after Jesus was killed on the cross, the priests still couldn't have what they desired. Envy is a murderous, traitorous spirit. We can never be prosperous while controlled by envy.

We can enjoy—but never covet—what others have. We should rejoice when others are blessed. We should be happy for them and at peace with them. If they let us enjoy what they have in some way, then we should enjoy it! Just remember that nothing truly belongs to any of us—everything belongs to the Lord— so there is no room for envy in our lives.

When I observe the material gain of others, I rejoice for them and pray that they will be able to experience true peace and joy *in spite of* their possessions.

"Rejoice with those who rejoice; mourn with those who mourn," the apostle Paul instructs us in Romans 12:15. We must never resent the blessings and prosperity of others. When I see someone else succeed and enjoy their success, I do not

When I observe the material gain of others, I rejoice for them and pray that they will be able to experience true peace and joy *in spite of* their possessions.

envy them. I truly take pleasure in their accomplishments. Conversely, when someone loses their possessions, whether it's in a southern California wildfire or a hurricane in the Bahamas, it grieves me. I want everyone to enjoy the blessings and prosperity of the Lord, and I want them to learn how to share these benefits with those in need.

UNFORGIVENESS

See to it that no one misses the grace of God and that no bitter root grows up to cause trouble and defile many.
(HEBREWS 12:15)

I believe that one of the biggest reasons I have been blessed is because I am a forgiver—a mercy giver. Like everyone in life, I have been hurt by others. On occasion I have been let down, put out, and trampled on. I have been misrepresented and misunderstood. I have been targeted by my enemies and betrayed by some people claiming to be my friends. If I wanted to hold a grudge, I could certainly find reason to do so. But I learned long ago that unforgiveness is a cancer. The only way to get rid of it is to cut it out—let go of it. The longer we hold on to it, the more it spreads, until finally we are eaten up by its rotten poison. There is only one option when it comes to treating this disease:

forgiveness! We must not allow the sins and offenses of others to cause us to sin.

In the same way that a person with a terminal illness does not prosper physically, a person with a spiritual illness will not prosper spiritually. As sinners saved by grace, we have received the mercy of Jesus Christ, who was crucified for our transgressions. Therefore, we must extend this mercy to others—even to those who have hurt us. Complete and total forgiveness is absolutely necessary in order to enjoy complete and genuine prosperity.

UNRESTRAINT

For the grace of God that brings salvation has appeared to all men. It teaches us to say "No" to ungodliness and worldly passions, and to live self-controlled, upright and godly lives in this present age. (TITUS 2:11-12)

Most people who find themselves in financial distress are there because of one thing: a lack of self-control. They desire worldly things and drive themselves into debt obtaining these things. Once in debt, they lack the self-discipline to make the necessary adjustments to get out of debt. One quality imparted by the fullness of the Holy Spirit is self-control, and this is essential in our lives.

Unrestraint leads to debt, and debt kills prosperity. If we do find ourselves in debt—even if it is not the result of irresponsible spending—we must be willing to adjust our spending in order to get out of debt. Self-discipline can be difficult, but the Lord respects our efforts to live a self-controlled lifestyle. God offers temperance (self-control) as a result of the Holy Spirit filling us and producing his fruit. In fact, even while we're working to satisfy a debt, we can experience true prosperity if we practice self-control. Conversely, unrestraint will disrupt the prosperity that God has in store for us.

IDOLATRY

Put to death, therefore, whatever belongs to your earthly nature: sexual immorality, impurity, lust, evil desires and greed, which is idolatry. (COLOSSIANS 3:5)

We must never allow anything but God and his will to capture our hearts. If something else captures our hearts, our thoughts, or our passions, it is an idol. For many men and women, their career becomes their idol. "Workaholics" are simply given over to occupational idolatry. When making money or earning status at the workplace becomes more important than the things of God, there can be no true prosperity. This is one situation where we often see material wealth without true prosperity. Career success without spiritual success or relational success is empty and without purpose. Certainly we were made to excel in business, but our success must be balanced in other meaningful ways. Proverbs 23:4 says, "Do not wear yourself out to get rich; have the wisdom to show restraint." When we strive for God's will and allow him to give us success at work, then we can have true prosperity.

Idolatry can also take the form of pleasure. There was a time in my life when I was completely wrapped up in the success of the Dallas Cowboys. As ridiculous as it sounds, I allowed my happiness to be determined by whether or not they won their games! Rather than enjoying football as a leisurely spectator sport, I allowed myself to be so carried away by the game that it actually became an idol in my life. The same thing can be true with hobbies—in my case golf and fishing—or anything else that takes priority over spiritual things. God gave us these things to enjoy, but when they become more important than the things of the Lord, they are idols. Ultimately they affect our sensitivity to God and others and diminish our spiritual discernment. Our relationship with God becomes clouded by the idols that stand between us. Idols must be cast down in order for us to prosper.

A third form of idolatry commonly seen in our society is materialism. When one becomes consumed with possessions—cars, houses, clothes, or anything else that is strictly material—then our focus shifts from spiritual things to worldly things.

Our relationship with God becomes clouded by the idols that stand between us. Idols must be cast down in order for us to prosper.

"Do not love the world or anything in the world. If anyone loves the world, the love of the Father is not in him" (1 John 2:15). Materialism makes earthly things the main pursuit of a person's heart. Although the Lord may bless his children with material gifts, much like a loving parent will shower his or her children with Christmas gifts, the love must stay focused on the giver of the gifts, not the gifts themselves. Imagine the reaction of a parent returning from a business trip, whose child asks, "What did you bring me?" If the parent responds, "I'm sorry, but I didn't have time to go shopping; I came directly home so I could be with you," and the child sulks off disappointed, the parent would naturally feel dejected and sad. However, if the child replies, "That's okay, I'm glad you're home!" then the parent would feel joy. Our heavenly Father is the same way—he wants us to be thrilled with his *presence,* not just his *presents!*

When we allow the things we possess to possess us instead, we have built an idol of materialism. As long as that idol stands, we will never truly prosper.

QUESTIONS & ANSWERS

Why couldn't the rich man in Jesus' parable enter heaven?

One of the most striking stories in the Gospels takes place when a powerful, wealthy man asks Jesus what he must do "to inherit eternal life." According to his own account, this man has obeyed the law; yet there was one thing missing in his life—total surrender to Christ, as represented in the area of his money.

> A certain ruler asked him, "Good teacher, what must I do to inherit eternal life?"
>
> "Why do you call me good?" Jesus answered. "No one is good—except God alone. You know the commandments: 'Do not commit adultery, do not murder, do not steal, do not give false testimony, honor your father and mother.'"
>
> "All these I have kept since I was a boy," he said.
>
> When Jesus heard this, he said to him, "You still lack one thing. Sell everything you have and give to the poor, and you will have treasure in heaven. Then come, follow me."

> *When he heard this, he became very sad, because he was a man of great wealth. Jesus looked at him and said, "How hard it is for the rich to enter the kingdom of God! Indeed, it is easier for a camel to go through the eye of a needle than for a rich man to enter the kingdom of God." Those who heard this asked, "Who then can be saved?"*
>
> *Jesus replied, "What is impossible with men is possible with God."*
>
> *Peter said to him, "We have left all we had to follow you!"*
>
> *"I tell you the truth," Jesus said to them, "no one who has left home or wife or brothers or parents or children for the sake of the kingdom of God will fail to receive many times as much in this age and, in the age to come, eternal life."*   (LUKE 18:18-30)

Many questions and answers arise from this incident. Those taking a vow of poverty point to the fact that Jesus told the man to give up everything in order to be saved. Prosperity preachers emphasize the fact that Jesus promised that the man would have received "many times as much in this age" had he given his money. One well-known minister writes, "He [Jesus] intended to give the rich young ruler a hundred times what he had!"[12]

Both of these extreme interpretations—the vow of poverty and the hundredfold increase—miss the point. On the one hand, if poverty paves the way to salvation, then why was the same measure not held to everyone Jesus encountered? Consider the story of Zacchaeus in the very next chapter of Luke:

> Jesus entered Jericho and was passing through. A man was there by the name of Zacchaeus; he was a chief tax collector and was wealthy. He wanted to see who Jesus was, but being a short man he could not, because of the crowd. So he ran ahead and climbed a sycamore-fig tree to see him, since Jesus was coming that way.
>
> When Jesus reached the spot, he looked up and said to him, "Zacchaeus, come down immediately. I must stay at your house today." So he came down at once and welcomed him gladly.
>
> All the people saw this and began to mutter, "He has gone to be the guest of a 'sinner.'"
>
> But Zacchaeus stood up and said to the Lord, "Look, Lord! Here and now I give half of my possessions to the poor, and if I have cheated anybody out of anything, I will pay back four times the amount."
>
> Jesus said to him, "Today salvation has come

to this house, because this man, too, is a son of
Abraham. For the Son of Man came to seek and
to save what was lost." (LUKE 19:1-10)

In this account Jesus visits the home of a known sinner—a man who apparently had cheated others to
obtain his wealth. After meeting with Jesus, Zacchaeus
promised to give *half* of his money to the poor and to
make quadruple restitution to those whom he had
cheated. Is Jesus being inconsistent by demanding *all*
of the rich young ruler's wealth, while being satisfied
with only half of Zacchaeus's? Likewise, in the parable
of the talents in Matthew 25, the servants who wisely
invested and multiplied the money entrusted to them
were commended as wise. If the servant who had bur-
ied his talent had simply given the money to the poor,
would he have been commended?

While recognizing and respecting our need for material things, Jesus illustrates that the poor are more
inclined to trust in God. Throughout Luke's narrative, it
is usually the poor who receive and respond to Jesus'
call. Acutely aware of their dependence and need, they
are most gratefully receptive to the Kingdom. By contrast, the wealthy are self-reliant, self-sufficient, and
self-satisfied. Their worldly possessions present a seemingly impossible obstacle to their spiritual growth.

Another interesting aspect of both passages—the account of the rich young ruler and that of Zacchaeus—is the fact that in neither case did Jesus demand that the money be given to him or his "organization." Jesus could easily have said, "Sell all your possessions and give the proceeds to Judas, my treasurer." After all, Jesus was feeding the hungry, healing the sick, and bringing salvation to the lost. What better ministry has ever existed on the face of the earth? Instead, in both cases, Jesus said to give the money "to the poor." What prosperity preacher has ever suggested that we make our vows to God and give our money directly to the poor?

What prosperity preacher has ever suggested that we make our vows to God and give our money directly to the poor?

The Scriptures clearly illustrate that "if anyone loves the world, the love of the Father is not in him" (1 John 2:15). Money can be an obstacle to our relationship with Jesus Christ. Before we can come to him, we must lay down every obstacle: "If anyone would come after me, he must deny himself and take up his cross daily and follow me. For whoever wants to save his life will lose it, but whoever loses his life for me will save it" (Luke 9:23-24).

Jesus told one man to sell everything he had and

give it to the poor. Others met Jesus' approval by giving only a portion of their money to those in need. Clearly the issue Jesus addressed was one of the heart, not one of the pocketbook. When money or possessions hold us back from pursuing the things of God, they must go. Idols must be cast down. Chains must be broken. By the grace of God, we must be overcomers. When we have been overcome by materialism, then we must allow the Lord to root out the source of our downfall and restore us in his image.

How do we best "tune in" to God's heart?

We need to tune our spiritual ears to clearly recognize and hear the voice of God. As I previously indicated, wherever you sit as you are reading these words, the room is filled with sound waves from many different sources: television stations in your community, satellite signals from outer space, and radio signals from around the world. Clear communication is available. The key is to tune in to the correct frequency to hear and see the messages as certainly as you can hear a loved one sitting across the room.

Properly tuning in also applies to the spiritual realm. By knowing God's written Word, it is possible to hear his clearly communicated spoken word. It has nothing to do with audible sound; it has everything to do with spiritual impact. God says in Proverbs 1:20-21, "Wisdom calls aloud in the street, she raises her voice in the public squares; at the head of the noisy streets she cries out, in the gateways of the city she makes her speech." Wisdom is clearly speaking to us, but do we hear it?

Sadly, few people even attempt to hear the Word of the Lord. Proverbs 8:1-3 says, "Does not wisdom call out? Does not understanding raise her voice? On the heights along the way, where the paths meet, she takes her stand; beside the gates leading into the city, at the entrances, she cries aloud." We need to tune our hearts, our minds, and our spiritual ears to hear and receive wisdom. The more we know the written Word, the more committed we will be to the God of the Word, and the more clearly we will hear his spiritual communication.

Previously, I shared how God led Betty and me to a piece of property that ultimately became monetarily profitable to us. We originally sought the property to find a place where our three children could grow up with a sense of security and room to play. Because my travel schedule at the time necessitated so much time away from home, I wanted to enjoy the time I had together with my family. We found a very inexpensive piece of property in an area that most people would have considered undesirable. For twenty-seven years, my friends asked me, "How can you live out here where the roads are like this?" One year ago the main road to our street was smoothly paved for the first time.

Today, our property is worth many times what we paid for it. However, you must hear this: Had the surrounding area never been developed, and had the property values stayed even or declined, our home still would have provided what God intended—the true prosperity that everyone desires to experience. We had a place for our family. A place for us to enjoy one another, to build meaningful relationships. We were seeking to do the will of God, and he poured his blessings on us—the blessings of an abundant life. We never expected it to produce a monetary abundance, but God chose to allow that as well.

> True prosperity is living in God's abiding presence, allowing him to fulfill his Kingdom purposes through us.

The miracle is not in the value of the property. The miracle is in the fact that even the monetary gain could not rob us of the priceless joy we experienced as a family living in that house—a joy that money can't buy. Regardless of our circumstances, we live in true prosperity. Regardless of our circumstances, we diligently seek to stay tuned in to God, to hear his voice, and to know his wisdom and understanding.

True prosperity is living in God's abiding presence, allowing him to fulfill his Kingdom purposes through us. When we have truly presented ourselves as living sacrifices (see Romans 12:1), God reveals his good, acceptable, and perfect will. Our yielded lives become lives fulfilled, and lives released—into true prosperity.

AFTERWORD

A Prayerful Commitment

I INVITE you to join me in this pledge:

Through God's enabling grace, I commit to put him first above all else and to care for others as I do for myself. I will honor God with the firstfruits of my increase and share my time and talents in ways to benefit others.

In all relationships I will always seek to give more than I could ever receive. I commit to have the heart of a farmer and trust God for the increase—by his means and in his timing. I will joyfully and faithfully give to God's Kingdom, helping the poor and those unable to help me, with no thought of return.

I will make all necessary changes to get out of bondage to debt, even if I must scale way down to ultimately step up. I will begin to live below my means. I will follow wise counsel and seek to tune my spiritual ears to hear the wisdom that comes only from above.

I will allow the river of God's life and love to flow freely through me, all to his glory.

Begin *now* by focusing on God first. Then find a need and meet it!

NOTES

1. Gregg Easterbrook, *The Progress Paradox: How Life Gets Better While People Feel Worse* (New York: Random House, 2003), quoted in Tim Madigan, "The Burden of Materialism," Fort Worth *Star-Telegram*, 17 March 2004, 1F.
2. David Myers, quoted in Madigan, "The Burden of Materialism."
3. Kalle Lasn, *Culture Jam: How to Reverse America's Suicidal Consumer Binge—and Why We Must* (New York: Quill, 2000), 5.
4. Madigan, "The Burden of Materialism."
5. Ibid.
6. Philip Yancey, *Soul Survivor* (New York: Doubleday, 2001), 115.
7. Ibid., 109–11.
8. Randy Alcorn, *Money, Possessions, and Eternity,* rev. ed. (Wheaton, Ill.: Tyndale, 2003), 306.
9. Matthew Henry, *Matthew Henry's Commentary on the Whole Bible,* (Peabody, Mass.: Hendrickson Publishers, 1991), Proverbs 22:16.
10. Kenneth Copeland, *The Laws of Prosperity* (Fort Worth, Tex.: Kenneth Copeland Publications, 1974), 63.
11. Merriam-Webster's Collegiate Dictionary, 11th ed., s.v. "envy."
12. Copeland, *The Laws of Prosperity,* 58.

ABOUT THE AUTHOR

James Robison, founder and president of Life Outreach International in Fort Worth, Texas, carries a great passion to communicate God's love in word and deed to people throughout the world. Life Outreach presently helps feed hundreds of thousands of children each month in Africa alone, while also caring for orphans and conducting relief efforts in eleven LIFE Centers on five continents. Life Outreach also drills water wells in many developing nations, providing clean drinking water for millions of people. During his forty years of ministry, more than twenty million people have heard James Robison preach as he conducted more than six hundred major citywide crusades and hundreds of church revivals. Many others have come to know him as one of America's most popular television talk-show hosts. *Life Today*, which he cohosts with his wife, Betty, airs throughout North America, Europe, and Australia. James and Betty have three grown children and eleven grandchildren.

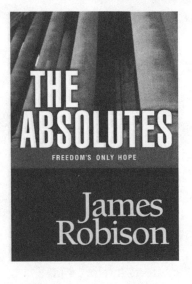